Homeschooling
WITH
HORSES

FUN-SCHOOLING JOURNAL
365 LEARNING ACTIVITIES & LESSONS

BY CHRISTINA EMILY BROWN
ALEXANDRA BRETUSH & SARAH JANISSE BROWN

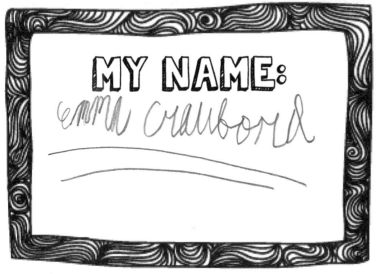

MY NAME:
emma crawford

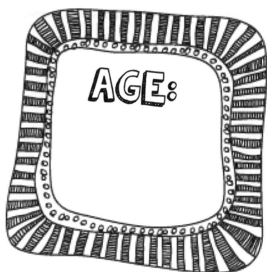

AGE:

ADDRESS:

ADDRESS:

Phone Number:

DATE:

INSTRUCTIONS

LIST or DRAW Eight THINGS
That you want to learn about:

1. How things are made
2. Horses
3. Dogs
4. Cats
5. Bees
6. _____
7. Soccer _____
8. _____

Action Steps:

1. Go to the library or bookstore.
2. Bring home a stack of at least EIGHT interesting books about these topics. Choose some that have diagrams, instructions and illustrations.

Supplies Needed:

You will need pencils, colored pencils, pens, markers and a new set of smooth black drawing pens for picture study and art exercises.

Choose Eight Books To Use As School Books!

1. Write down the titles on each cover below.
2. Keep your stack of books in a safe place.
3. Be ready to read a few pages from your books daily.
4. Complete 10 pages each day in this workbook. Start each day on the date page.

CIRCLE TODAY'S DATE

January
February
March
April
May
June
July
(August)
September
October
November
December

1 2 3 4 5 6
7 8 (9) (10) 11
12 13 14 15
16 17 18 19
20 21 22 23
24 25 26 27
28 29 30 31

MONDAY
TUESDAY
WEDNESDAY
THURSDAY
FRIDAY
SATURDAY
SUNDAY

2018
2019
2020
2021
2022
(2023)
2024
2025
2026
2027
2028
2029
2030
2031

Write Today's Date: __8/9/23, wednesday__ (and 10/3/23, tuesday)

10

FEELINGS, PLANS & THOUGHTS

Copy a Quote or Verse:

rejoice in the Lord always; again
I will say, rejoice.

— phillippians 4:4

Draw a picture about your feelings:

To-Do List

Teach Max settle

Teach Larry sit.

Reading Time - 1 Hour (Set a Timer)

Choose Four Books - Read from each book for 15 minutes.
Copy important words and pictures from your books:

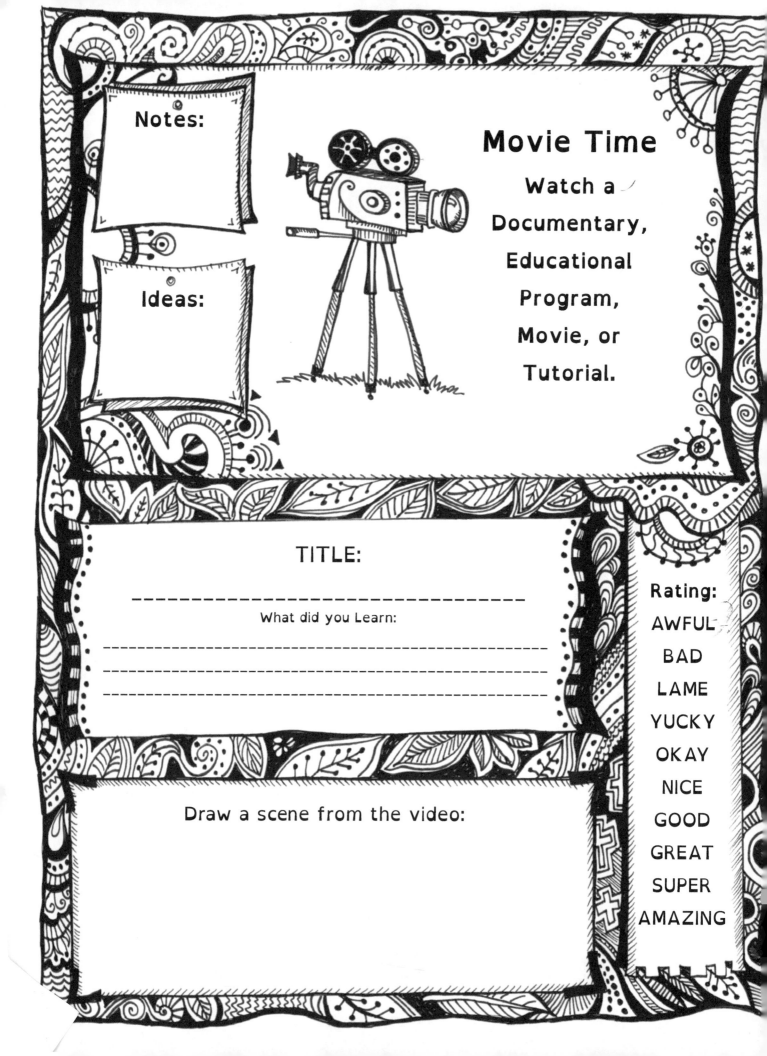

Notes:

Ideas:

Movie Time

Watch a Documentary, Educational Program, Movie, or Tutorial.

TITLE:

_____

What did you Learn:

Draw a scene from the video:

Rating:

AWFUL

BAD

LAME

YUCKY

OKAY

NICE

GOOD

GREAT

SUPER

AMAZING

MATH & CREATIVITY

Use this page for math problems

or design something like a house, farm or stable!

$5 \times 6 = 30$

$3 \times 4 = 12$

$2 \times 8 = 16$

$10 \times 10 = 100$

$12 \times 4 = 48$

$1 \times 0 = 0$

$7 \times 11 = 77$

$4 \div 2 = 2$

$6 \div 3 = 2$

$5 \div 1 = 5$

$12 \div 3 = 4$

$10 \div 2 = 5$

$8 \div 1 = 8$

$9 \div 3 = 3$

World News Today!

Talk to your parents about current events.

Look at a newspaper, news broadcast or website.

Color the countries you learn about.

Tell the news stories with words or pictures.

_____

_____

ALL ABOUT HORSES:

Choose a Horse Breed to Research:

_____

List Four Facts about this Breed:

1._____
_____
2._____
_____
3._____
_____
4._____
_____

DRAW THIS TYPE OF HORSE OR TAPE A PICTURE HERE:

Picture Study

Look closely at this picture.

Think about the lines and shadows.

Practice working with your colored pencils.

Draw the Missing Spot

Use a variety of smooth black drawing pens,
with fine points, to complete the picture.

CIRCLE TODAY'S DATE

January
February
March
April
May
June
July
August
September
October
November
December

1 2 3 4 5 6
7 8 9 10 11
12 13 14 15
16 17 18 19
20 21 22 23
24 25 26 27
28 29 30 31

MONDAY
TUESDAY
WEDNESDAY
THURSDAY
FRIDAY
SATURDAY
SUNDAY

2018
2019
2020
2021
2022
2023
2024
2025
2026
2027
2028
2029
2030
2031

Write Today's Date: 1/29/24

FEELINGS, PLANS & THOUGHTS

Copy a Quote or Verse:

Teach me thy ways, o'Lord, shew me thy paths.

Draw a picture about your feelings:

To-Do List
- Play w/ Violet
- Make doll-Movie
- Discuss FLOWER CLUB!

21

NATURE STUDY

Go outside and make a realistic drawing
of something you find in nature.

Reading Time - 1 Hour (Set a Timer)

Choose Four Books - Read from each book for 15 minutes.

Copy important words and pictures from your books:

Spelling Time

Find 20 Words with **5** letters each.
Look in your books for words.
Write the words here:

Horse

Movie

Weird

Super

Human

Scene

Title

learn

Goofy

Spell

Bloom

Start

Heart

Books

Katie

Maddy

Elsie

Daisy

Daily

Shoes

Notes:

Ideas:

Movie Time

Watch a Documentary, Educational Program, Movie, or Tutorial.

TITLE:

_____

What did you Learn:

_____
_____
_____

Draw a scene from the video:

Rating:

AWFUL

BAD

LAME

YUCKY

OKAY

NICE

GOOD

GREAT

SUPER

AMAZING

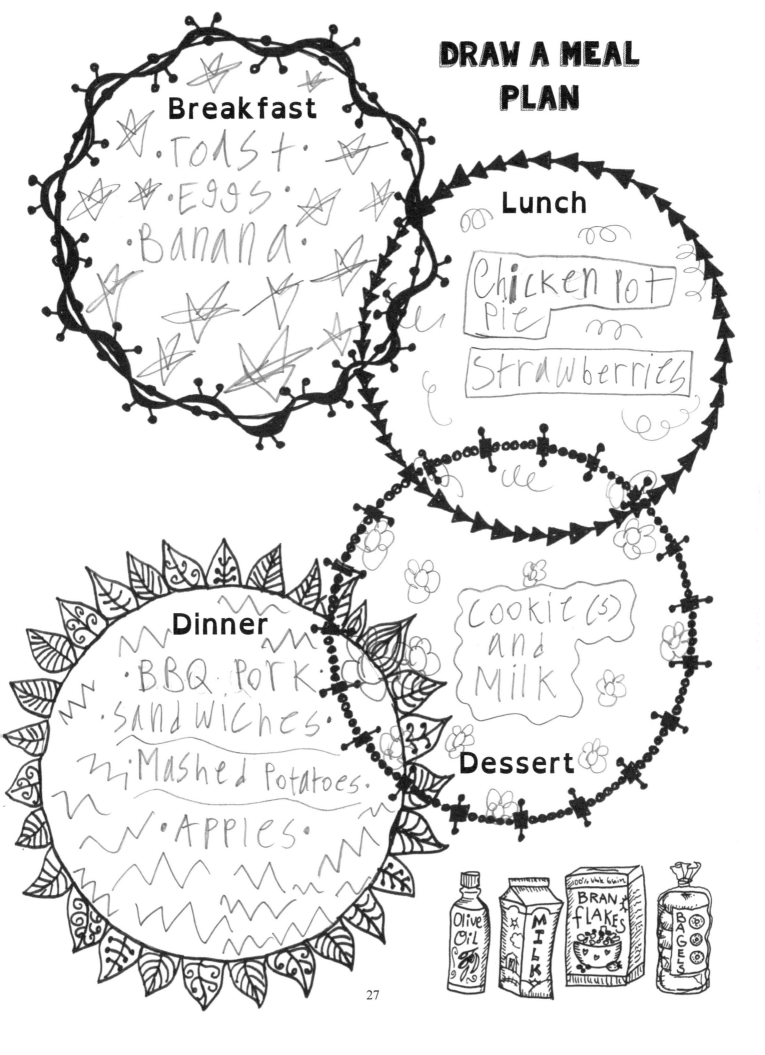

DRAW A MEAL PLAN

Breakfast
Toast
Eggs
Banana

Lunch
Chicken Pot Pie
Strawberries

Dinner
· B.B.Q. Pork ·
· Sandwiches ·
· Mashed Potatoes ·
· Apples ·

Dessert
Cookie (s) and Milk

Olive Oil

MILK

BRAN FLAKES

BAGELS

27

ALL ABOUT HORSES:

Choose a Horse Breed to Research:

_____

List Four Facts about this Breed:

1._____
_____
2._____
_____
3._____
_____
4._____
_____

DRAW THIS TYPE OF HORSE OR TAPE A PICTURE HERE:

CIRCLE TODAY'S DATE

(January)
February
March
April
May
June
July
August
September
October
November
December

1 2 3 4 5 6
7 8 9 10 11
12 13 14 15
16 17 18 19
20 21 22 23
24 25 26 27
28 29 30 (31)

MONDAY
TUESDAY
(WEDNESDAY)
THURSDAY
FRIDAY
SATURDAY
SUNDAY

2018
2019
2020
2021
2022
2023
(2024)
2025
2026
2027
2028
2029
2030
2031

Write Today's Date: _1/31/24_ _ _ _ _ _ _ _ _

30

FEELINGS, PLANS & THOUGHTS

Copy a Quote or Verse:

Draw a picture
about your feelings:

To-Do List

_____

_____

_____

_____

_____

_____

NATURE STUDY

Go outside and make a realistic drawing
of something you find in nature.

Reading Time - 1 Hour (Set a Timer)

Choose Four Books - Read from each book for 15 minutes.

Copy important words and pictures from your books:

Spelling Time

Find 20 Words with **6** letters each.
Look in your books for words.
Write the words here:

_____ _____

_____ _____

_____ _____

_____ _____

_____ _____

_____ _____

_____ _____

_____ _____

_____ _____

_____ _____

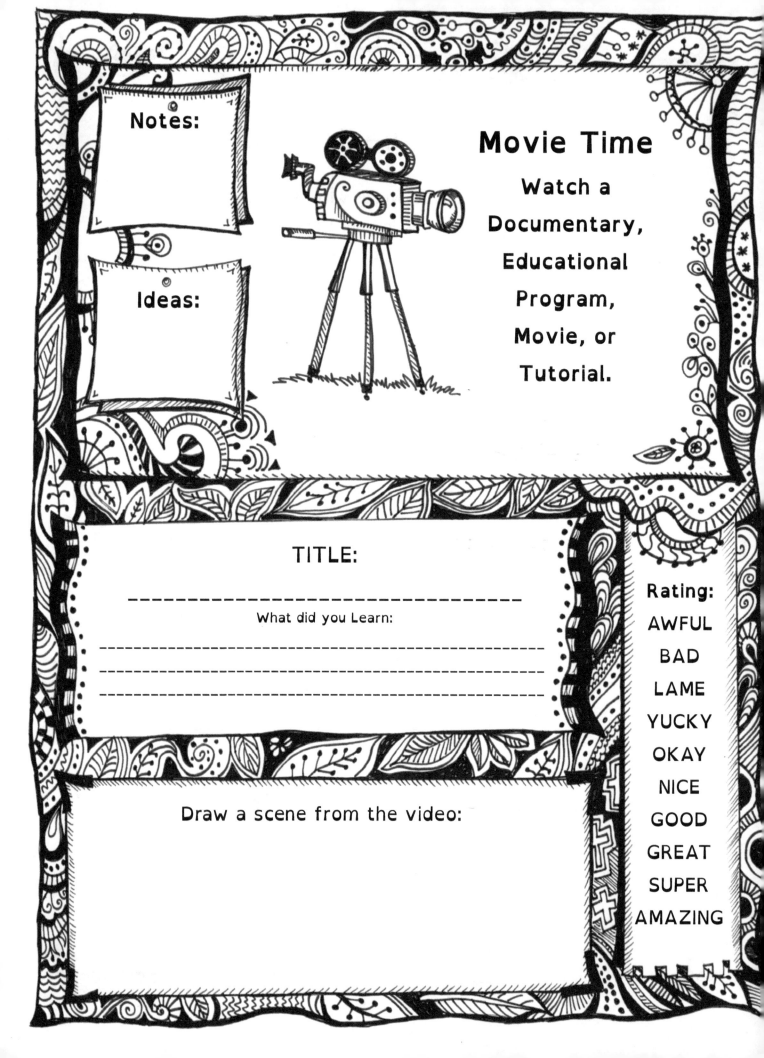

Notes:

Ideas:

Movie Time

Watch a Documentary, Educational Program, Movie, or Tutorial.

TITLE:

_____

What did you Learn:

_____
_____
_____

Draw a scene from the video:

Rating:

AWFUL

BAD

LAME

YUCKY

OKAY

NICE

GOOD

GREAT

SUPER

AMAZING

MATH & CREATIVITY

Use this page for math problems
or design something like a house, farm or stable!

ALL ABOUT HORSES:

Choose a Horse Breed to Research:

_____

List Four Facts about this Breed:

1._____
_____
2._____
_____
3._____
_____
4._____
_____

DRAW THIS TYPE OF HORSE OR TAPE A PICTURE HERE:

CIRCLE TODAY'S DATE

January
(February)
March
April
May
June
July
August
September
October
November
December

(1) 2 3 4 5 6
7 8 9 10 11
12 13 14 15
16 17 18 19
20 21 22 23
24 25 26 27
28 29 30 31

MONDAY
TUESDAY
WEDNESDAY
(THURSDAY)
FRIDAY
SATURDAY
SUNDAY

2018
2019
2020
2021
2022
2023
(2024)
2025
2026
2027
2028
2029
2030
2031

Write Today's Date: 2/1/24 _ _ _ _ _ _ _ _

40

FEELINGS, PLANS & THOUGHTS

Copy a Quote or Verse:

_____
_____
_____
_____
_____
_____

Draw a picture
about your feelings:

To-Do List

_____
_____
_____
_____
_____

Create a Comic Strip!

Practice Using Your Pens

Picture Study

Look closely at this picture.

Think about the lines and shadows.

Practice working with your colored pencils.

Draw the Missing Spot

Use a variety of smooth black drawing pens,
with fine points, to complete the picture.

Reading Time - 1 Hour (Set a Timer)

Choose Four Books - Read from each book for 15 minutes.

Copy important words and pictures from your books:

Spelling Time

Find 20 Words with 7 letters each.
Look in your books for words.
Write the words here:

_____   _____

_____   _____

_____   _____

_____   _____

_____   _____

_____   _____

_____   _____

_____   _____

_____   _____

_____   _____

Notes:

Ideas:

Movie Time

Watch a Documentary, Educational Program, Movie, or Tutorial.

TITLE:

_____

What did you Learn:

- -
- -
- -

Rating:
AWFUL
BAD
LAME
YUCKY
OKAY
NICE
GOOD
GREAT
SUPER
AMAZING

Draw a scene from the video:

CIRCLE TODAY'S DATE

January
(February)
March
April
May
June
July
August
September
October
November
December

1 (2) 3 4 5 6
7 8 9 10 11
12 13 14 15
16 17 18 19
20 21 22 23
24 25 26 27
28 29 30 31

MONDAY
TUESDAY
WEDNESDAY
THURSDAY
(FRIDAY)
SATURDAY
SUNDAY

2018
2019
2020
2021
2022
2023
(2024)
2025
2026
2027
2028
2029
2030
2031

Write Today's Date: 2/2/24

FEELINGS, PLANS & THOUGHTS

Copy a Quote or Verse:

_____
_____
_____
_____
_____
_____

Draw a picture
about your feelings:

To-Do List

_____
_____
_____
_____
_____
_____

MATH & CREATIVITY

Use this page for math problems

or design something like a house, farm or stable!

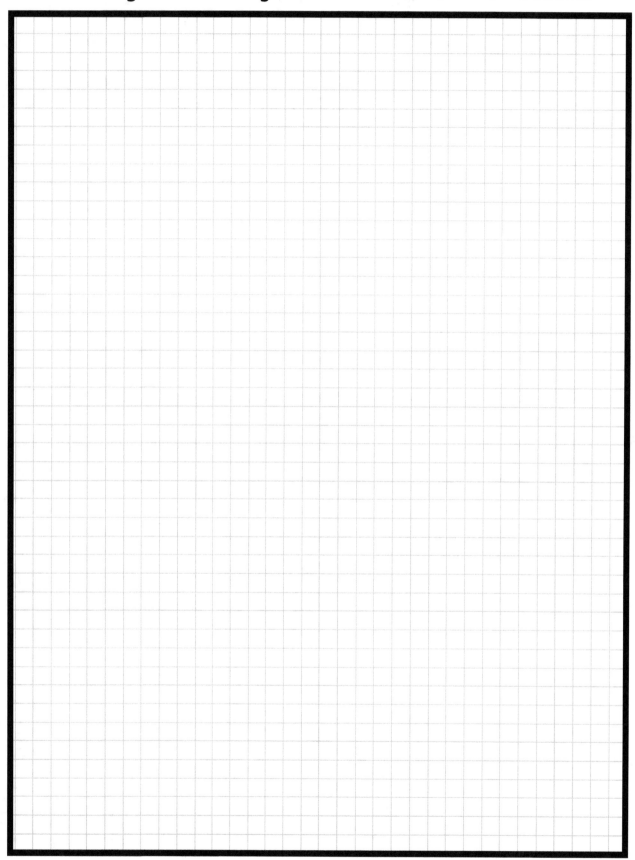

Picture Study

Look closely at this picture.

Think about the lines and shadows.

Practice working with your colored pencils.

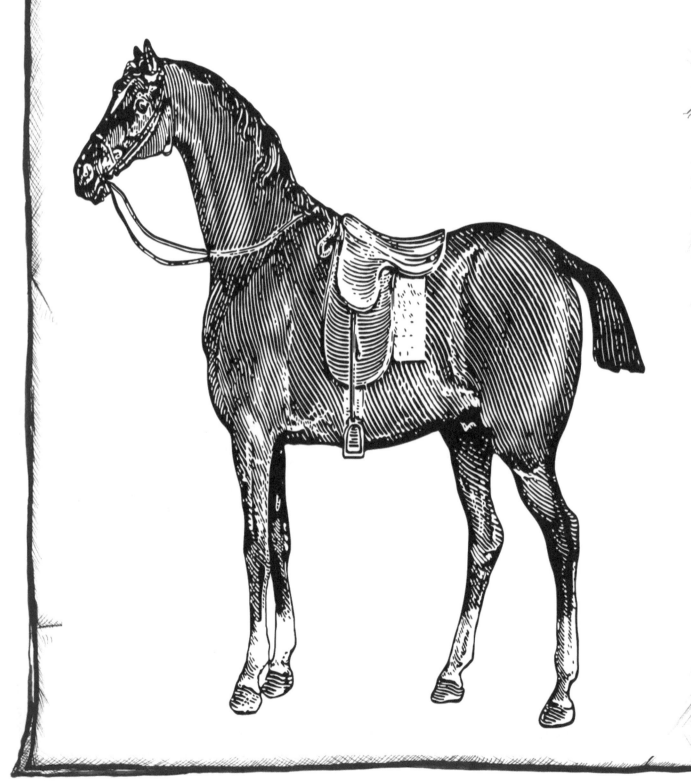

Draw the Missing Spot

Use a variety of smooth black drawing pens,
with fine points, to complete the picture.

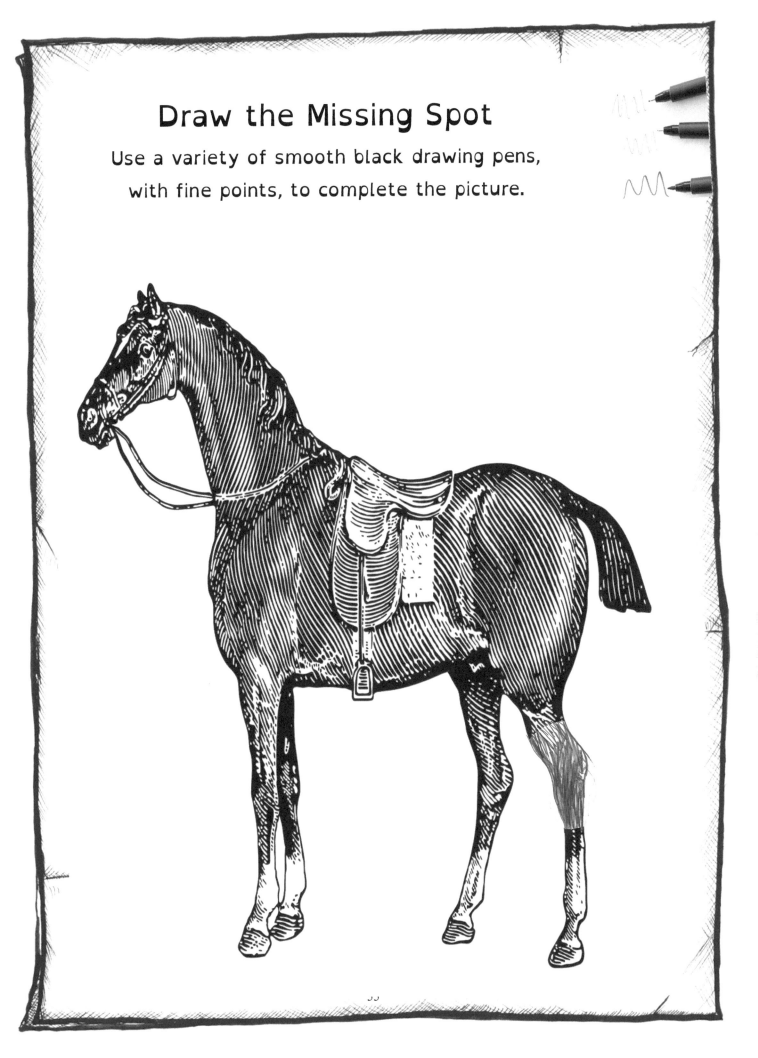

NATURE STUDY

Go outside and make a realistic drawing
of something you find in nature.

Reading Time - 1 Hour (Set a Timer)

Choose Four Books - Read from each book for 15 minutes.

Copy important words and pictures from your books:

Spelling Time

Find 20 Words with **8** letters each.

Look in your books for words.

Write the words here:

_____   _____

_____   _____

_____   _____

_____   _____

_____   _____

_____   _____

_____   _____

_____   _____

_____   _____

_____   _____

58

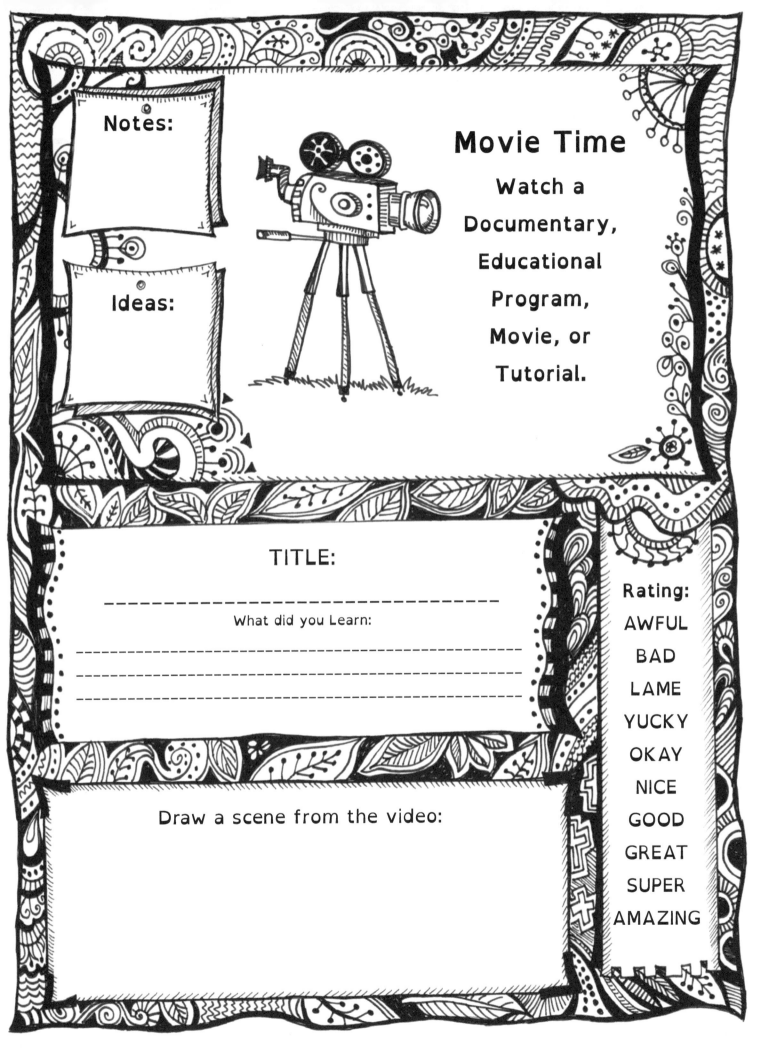

Notes:

Ideas:

Movie Time

Watch a Documentary, Educational Program, Movie, or Tutorial.

TITLE:

_____

What did you Learn:

_____
_____
_____

Rating:

AWFUL

BAD

LAME

YUCKY

OKAY

NICE

GOOD

GREAT

SUPER

AMAZING

Draw a scene from the video:

MATH & CREATIVITY

Use this page for math problems
or design something like a house, farm or stable!

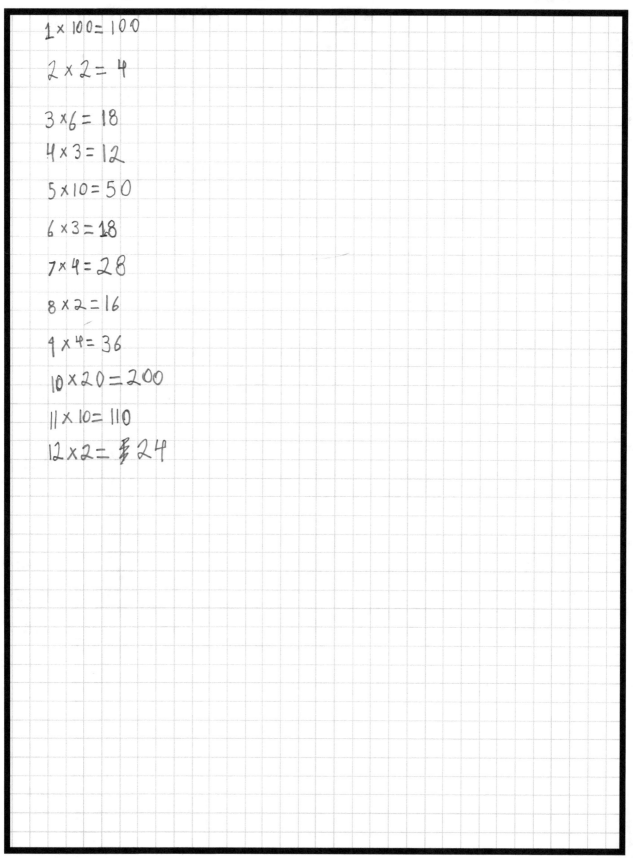

$1 \times 100 = 100$

$2 \times 2 = 4$

$3 \times 6 = 18$

$4 \times 3 = 12$

$5 \times 10 = 50$

$6 \times 3 = 18$

$7 \times 4 = 28$

$8 \times 2 = 16$

$9 \times 4 = 36$

$10 \times 20 = 200$

$11 \times 10 = 110$

$12 \times 2 = 24$

CIRCLE TODAY'S DATE

January
February
March
April
May
June
(July)
August
September
October
November
December

1 2 3 4 5 6
7 8 (9) 10 11
12 13 14 15
16 17 18 19
20 21 22 23
24 25 26 27
28 29 30 31

MONDAY
(TUESDAY)
WEDNESDAY
THURSDAY
FRIDAY
SATURDAY
SUNDAY

2018
2019
2020
2021
2022
2023
(2024)
2025
2026
2027
2028
2029
2030
2031

Write Today's Date: __7/9/2024_____

FEELINGS, PLANS & THOUGHTS

Copy a Quote or Verse:

_____

_____

_____

_____

_____

_____

Draw a picture about your feelings:

To-Do List

_____

_____

_____

_____

_____

_____

Picture Study

Look closely at this picture.

Think about the lines and shadows.

Practice working with your colored pencils.

Draw the Missing Spot

Use a variety of smooth black drawing pens,
with fine points, to complete the picture.

Reading Time - 1 Hour (Set a Timer)

Choose Four Books - Read from each book for 15 minutes.

Copy important words and pictures from your books:

Create a Comic Strip!

Spelling Time

Find 20 Words with 9 letters each.

Look in your books for words.

Write the words here:

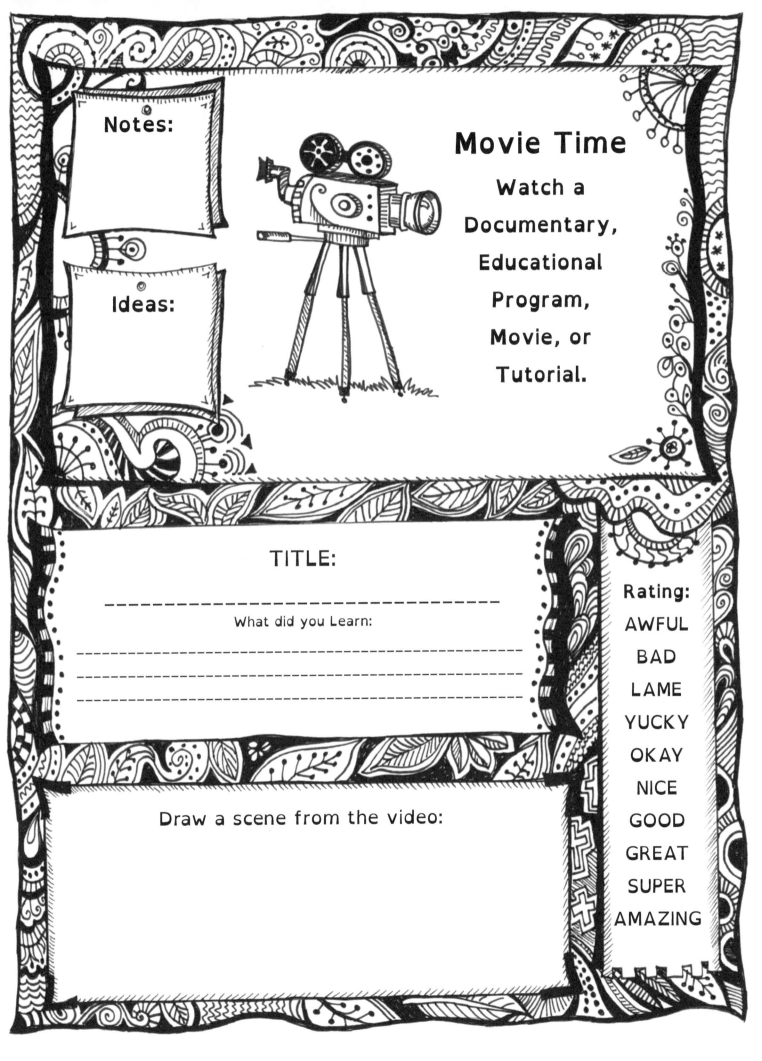

Notes:

Ideas:

Movie Time

Watch a Documentary, Educational Program, Movie, or Tutorial.

TITLE:

_____

What did you Learn:

_____
_____
_____

Draw a scene from the video:

Rating:

AWFUL

BAD

LAME

YUCKY

OKAY

NICE

GOOD

GREAT

SUPER

AMAZING

CIRCLE TODAY'S DATE

January
February
March
April
May
June
July
August
September
October
November
December

1 2 3 4 5 6
7 8 9 10 11
12 13 14 15
16 17 18 19
20 21 22 23
24 25 26 27
28 29 30 31

MONDAY
TUESDAY
WEDNESDAY
THURSDAY
FRIDAY
SATURDAY
SUNDAY

2018
2019
2020
2021
2022
2023
2024
2025
2026
2027
2028
2029
2030
2031

Write Today's Date:_ _ _ _ _ _ _ _ _ _ _ _ _ _

FEELINGS, PLANS & THOUGHTS

Copy a Quote or Verse:

_____

_____

_____

_____

_____

_____

Draw a picture
about your feelings:

To-Do List

_____

_____

_____

_____

_____

_____

MATH & CREATIVITY

Use this page for math problems

or design something like a house, farm or stable!

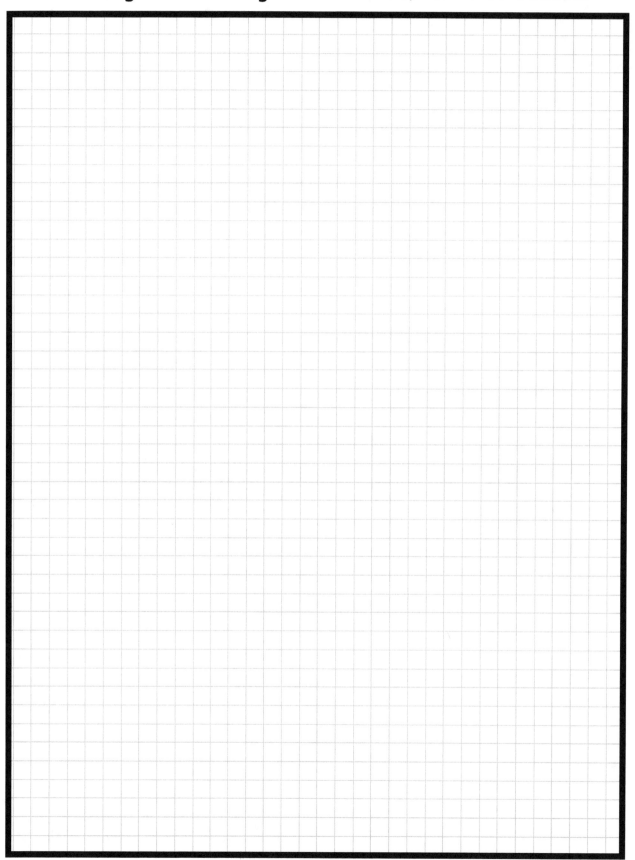

World News Today!

Talk to your parents about current events.

Look at a newspaper, news broadcast or website.

Color the countries you learn about.

Tell the news stories with words or pictures.

ALL ABOUT HORSES:

Choose a Horse Breed to Research:

_____

List Four Facts about this Breed:

1._____
_____
2._____
_____
3._____
_____
4._____
_____

DRAW THIS TYPE OF HORSE OR TAPE A PICTURE HERE:

Create a Comic Strip!

Picture Study

Look closely at this picture.

Think about the lines and shadows.

Practice working with your colored pencils.

Draw the Missing Spot

Use a variety of smooth black drawing pens,
with fine points, to complete the picture.

NATURE STUDY

Go outside and make a realistic drawing
of something you find in nature.

Reading Time - 1 Hour (Set a Timer)

Choose Four Books - Read from each book for 15 minutes.

Copy important words and pictures from your books:

CIRCLE TODAY'S DATE

January
February
March
April
May
June
July
August
September
October
November
December

1 2 3 4 5 6
7 8 9 10 11
12 13 14 15
16 17 18 19
20 21 22 23
24 25 26 27
28 29 30 31

MONDAY
TUESDAY
WEDNESDAY
THURSDAY
FRIDAY
SATURDAY
SUNDAY

2018
2019
2020
2021
2022
2023
2024
2025
2026
2027
2028
2029
2030
2031

Write Today's Date: _ _ _ _ _ _ _ _ _ _ _ _ _ _ _

FEELINGS, PLANS & THOUGHTS

Copy a Quote or Verse:

_____

_____

_____

_____

_____

_____

Draw a picture
about your feelings:

To-Do List

_____

_____

_____

_____

_____

_____

Spelling Time

Find 20 Words with **8** letters each.
Look in your books for words.
Write the words here:

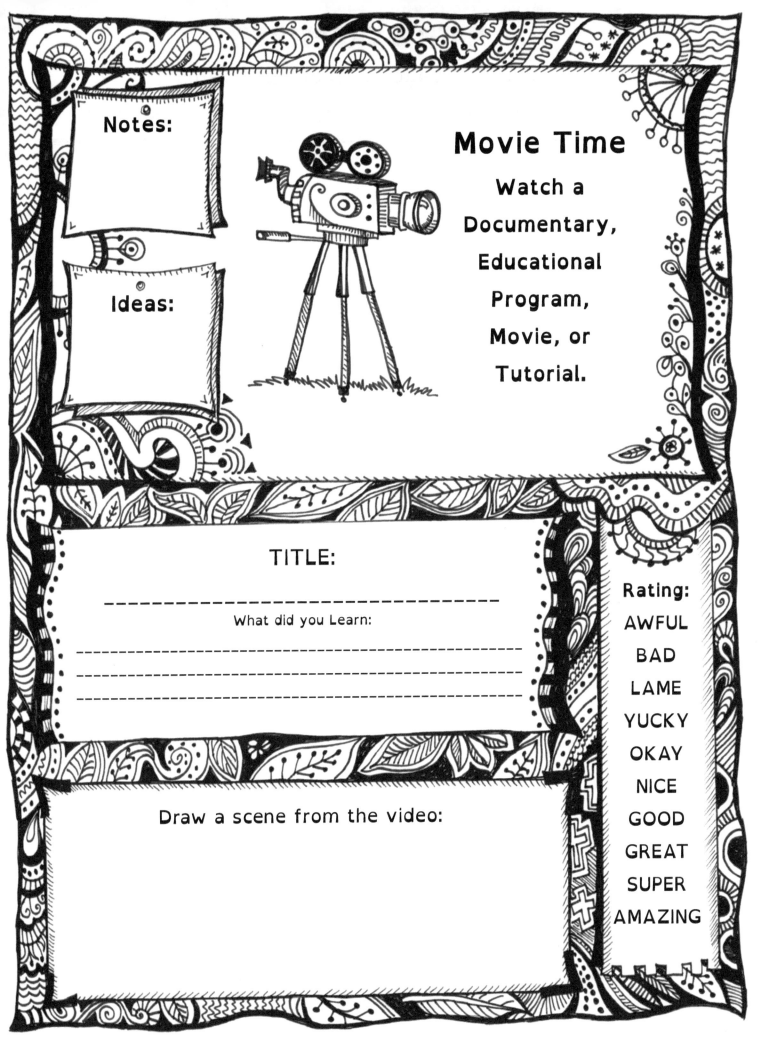

Notes:

Ideas:

Movie Time

Watch a Documentary, Educational Program, Movie, or Tutorial.

TITLE:

_____

What did you Learn:

_____
_____
_____

Draw a scene from the video:

Rating:
AWFUL
BAD
LAME
YUCKY
OKAY
NICE
GOOD
GREAT
SUPER
AMAZING

MATH & CREATIVITY

Use this page for math problems
or design something like a house, farm or stable!

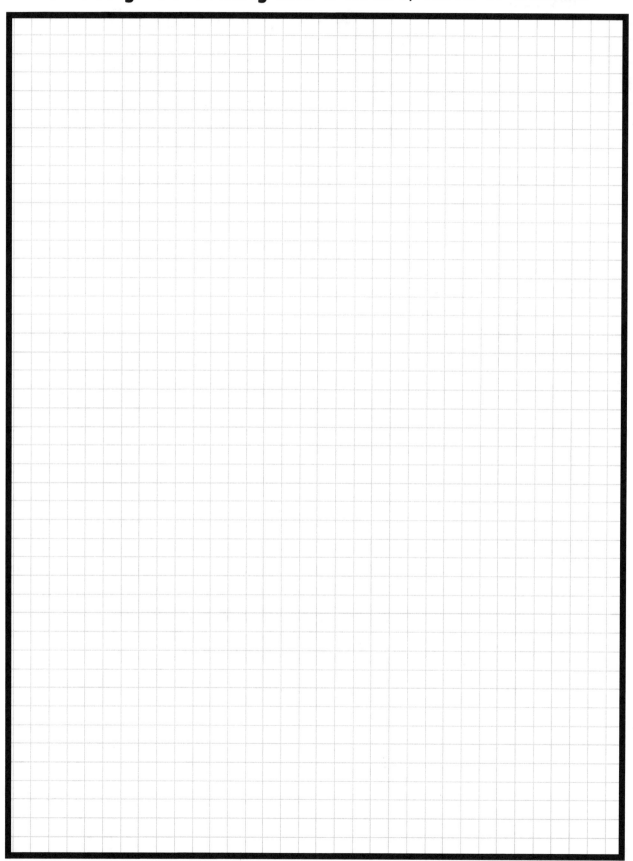

ALL ABOUT HORSES:

Choose a Horse Breed to Research:

_____

List Four Facts about this Breed:

1._____
_____
2._____
_____
3._____
_____
4._____
_____

DRAW THIS TYPE OF HORSE OR TAPE A PICTURE HERE:

Picture Study

Look closely at this picture.

Think about the lines and shadows.

Practice working with your colored pencils.

Draw the Missing Spot

Use a variety of smooth black drawing pens,
with fine points, to complete the picture.

CIRCLE TODAY'S DATE

January
February
March
April
May
June
July
August
September
October
November
December

1 2 3 4 5 6
7 8 9 10 11
12 13 14 15
16 17 18 19
20 21 22 23
24 25 26 27
28 29 30 31

MONDAY
TUESDAY
WEDNESDAY
THURSDAY
FRIDAY
SATURDAY
SUNDAY

2018
2019
2020
2021
2022
2023
2024
2025
2026
2027
2028
2029
2030
2031

Write Today's Date: _ _ _ _ _ _ _ _ _ _ _ _ _

FEELINGS, PLANS & THOUGHTS

Copy a Quote or Verse:

_____
_____
_____
_____
_____
_____

Draw a picture
about your feelings:

To-Do List

_____
_____
_____
_____
_____
_____

Reading Time - 1 Hour (Set a Timer)

Choose Four Books - Read from each book for 15 minutes.

Copy important words and pictures from your books:

Spelling Time

Find 20 Words with 7 letters each.

Look in your books for words.

Write the words here:

_____   _____

_____   _____

_____   _____

_____   _____

_____   _____

_____   _____

_____   _____

_____   _____

_____   _____

Notes:

Ideas:

Movie Time

Watch a Documentary, Educational Program, Movie, or Tutorial.

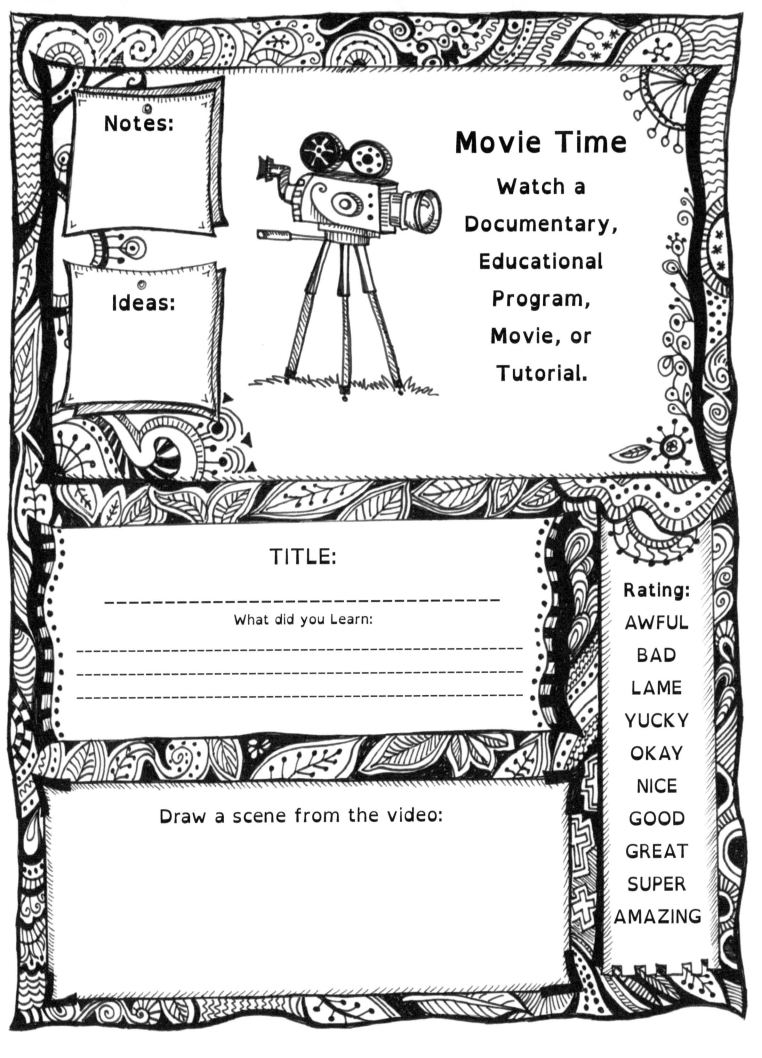

TITLE:

_____

What did you Learn:

_____
_____
_____

Draw a scene from the video:

Rating:
AWFUL
BAD
LAME
YUCKY
OKAY
NICE
GOOD
GREAT
SUPER
AMAZING

MATH & CREATIVITY

Use this page for math problems
or design something like a house, farm or stable!

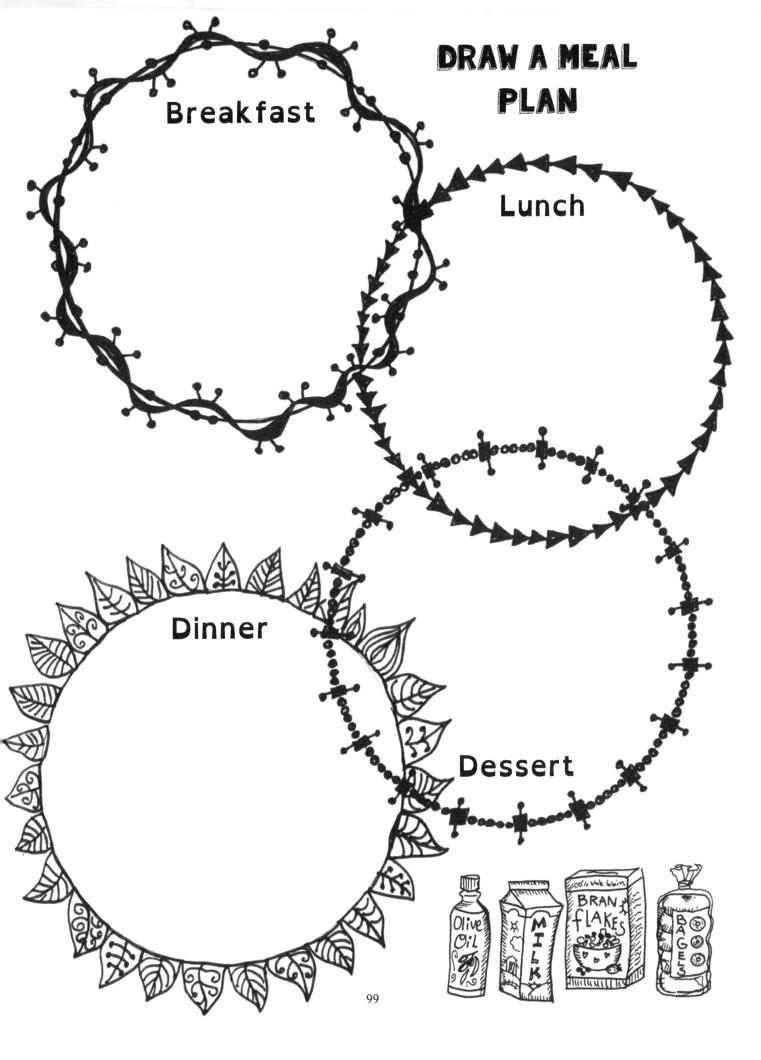

DRAW A MEAL
PLAN

Breakfast

Lunch

Dinner

Dessert

99

ALL ABOUT HORSES:

Choose a Horse Breed to Research:

_____

List Four Facts about this Breed:

1._____
_____
2._____
_____
3._____
_____
4._____
_____

DRAW THIS TYPE OF HORSE OR TAPE A PICTURE HERE:

Create a Comic Strip!

CIRCLE TODAY'S DATE

January
February
March
April
May
June
July
August
September
October
November
December

1 2 3 4 5 6
7 8 9 10 11
12 13 14 15
16 17 18 19
20 21 22 23
24 25 26 27
28 29 30 31

MONDAY
TUESDAY
WEDNESDAY
THURSDAY
FRIDAY
SATURDAY
SUNDAY

2018
2019
2020
2021
2022
2023
2024
2025
2026
2027
2028
2029
2030
2031

Write Today's Date:_ _ _ _ _ _ _ _ _ _ _ _

FEELINGS, PLANS & THOUGHTS

Copy a Quote or Verse:

_____

_____

_____

_____

_____

_____

Draw a picture about your feelings:

To-Do List

_____

_____

_____

_____

_____

_____

Picture Study

Look closely at this picture.

Think about the lines and shadows.

Practice working with your colored pencils.

Draw the Missing Spot

Use a variety of smooth black drawing pens,
with fine points, to complete the picture.

NATURE STUDY

Go outside and make a realistic drawing
of something you find in nature.

Reading Time - 1 Hour (Set a Timer)

Choose Four Books - Read from each book for 15 minutes.

Copy important words and pictures from your books:

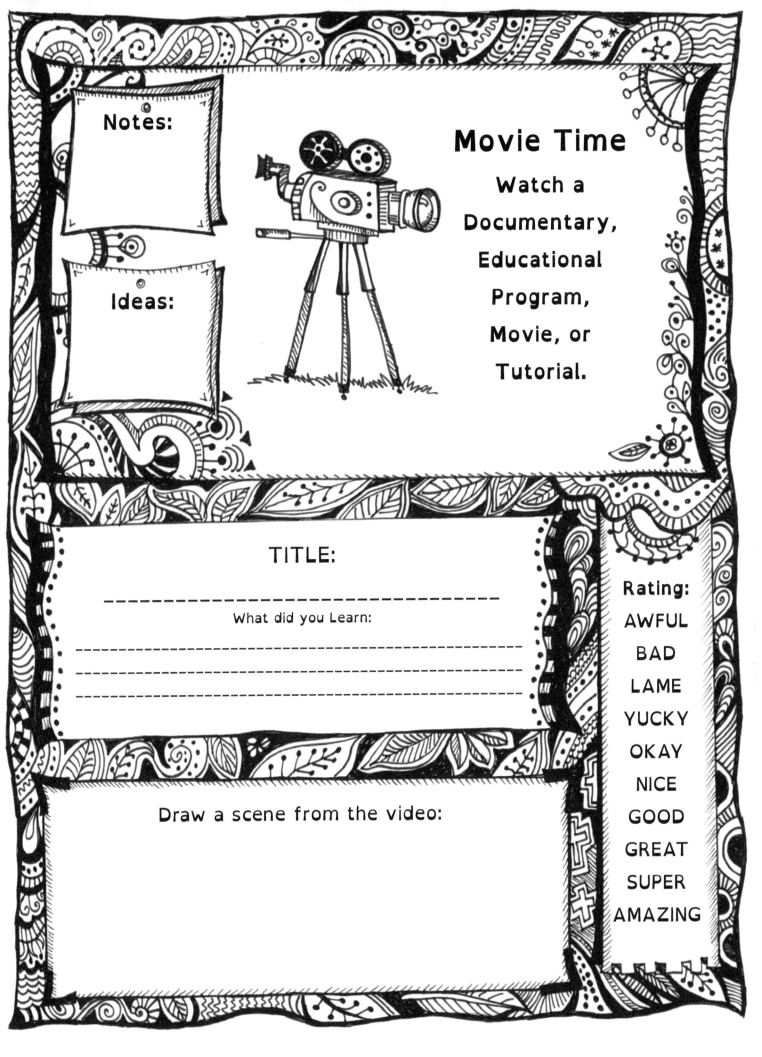

Notes:

Ideas:

Movie Time

Watch a Documentary, Educational Program, Movie, or Tutorial.

TITLE:

_____

What did you Learn:

_____
_____
_____

Rating:
AWFUL
BAD
LAME
YUCKY
OKAY
NICE
GOOD
GREAT
SUPER
AMAZING

Draw a scene from the video:

MATH & CREATIVITY
Use this page for math problems
or design something like a house, farm or stable!

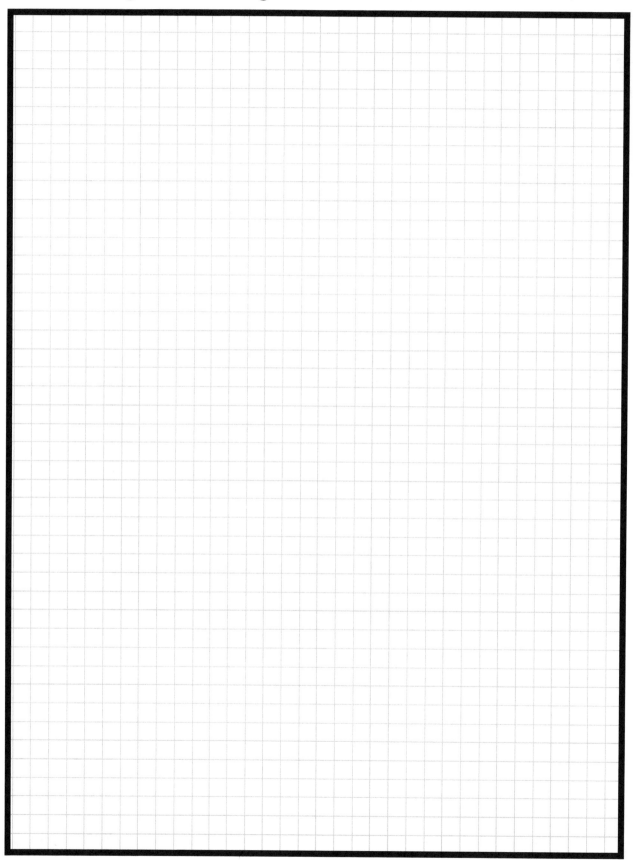

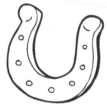

ALL ABOUT HORSES:

Choose a Horse Breed to Research:

_____

List Four Facts about this Breed:

1._____
_____
2._____
_____
3._____
_____
4._____
_____

DRAW THIS TYPE OF HORSE OR TAPE A PICTURE HERE:

CIRCLE TODAY'S DATE

January
February
March
April
May
June
July
August
September
October
November
December

1 2 3 4 5 6
7 8 9 10 11
12 13 14 15
16 17 18 19
20 21 22 23
24 25 26 27
28 29 30 31

MONDAY
TUESDAY
WEDNESDAY
THURSDAY
FRIDAY
SATURDAY
SUNDAY

2018
2019
2020
2021
2022
2023
2024
2025
2026
2027
2028
2029
2030
2031

Write Today's Date: _ _ _ _ _ _ _ _ _ _ _ _ _ _ _ _

FEELINGS, PLANS & THOUGHTS

Copy a Quote or Verse:

_____
_____
_____
_____
_____
_____

Draw a picture
about your feelings:

To-Do List

_____
_____
_____
_____
_____

Picture Study

Look closely at this picture.

Think about the lines and shadows.

Practice working with your colored pencils.

Draw the Missing Spot

Use a variety of smooth black drawing pens,
with fine points, to complete the picture.

NATURE STUDY

Go outside and make a realistic drawing
of something you find in nature.

Reading Time - 1 Hour (Set a Timer)

Choose Four Books - Read from each book for 15 minutes.
Copy important words and pictures from your books:

Spelling Time

Find 20 Words with 5 letters each.

Look in your books for words.

Write the words here:

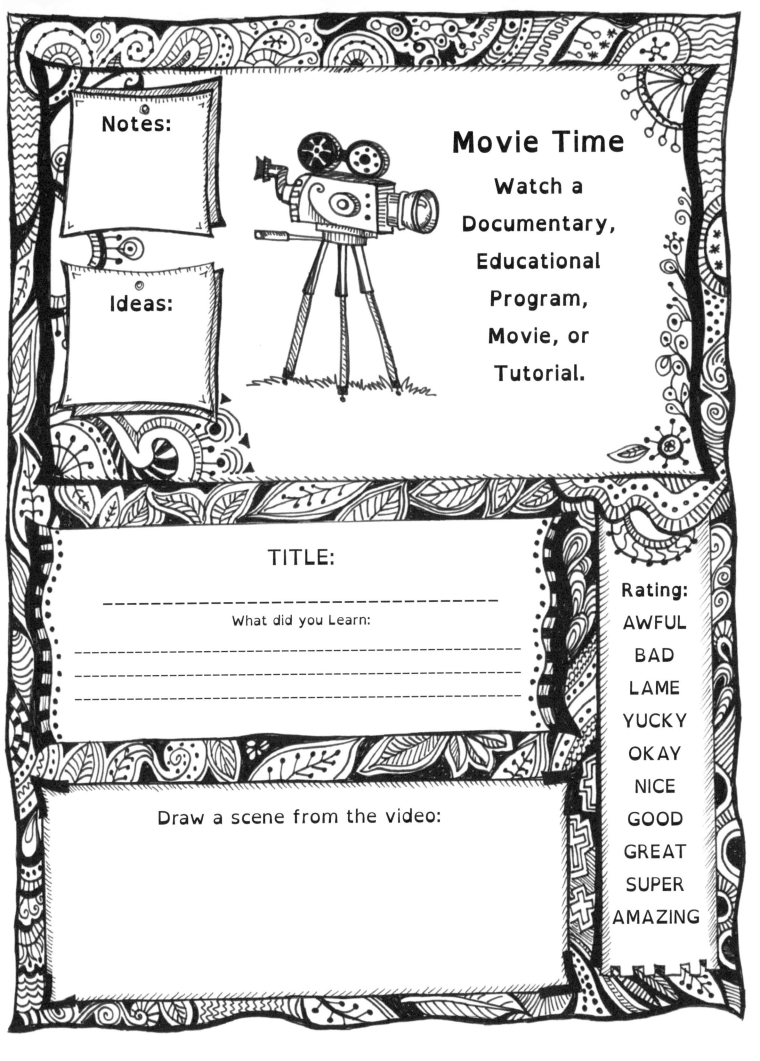

Notes:

Ideas:

Movie Time

Watch a Documentary, Educational Program, Movie, or Tutorial.

TITLE:

_____

What did you Learn:

_____
_____
_____

Draw a scene from the video:

Rating:
AWFUL
BAD
LAME
YUCKY
OKAY
NICE
GOOD
GREAT
SUPER
AMAZING

MATH & CREATIVITY

Use this page for math problems

or design something like a house, farm or stable!

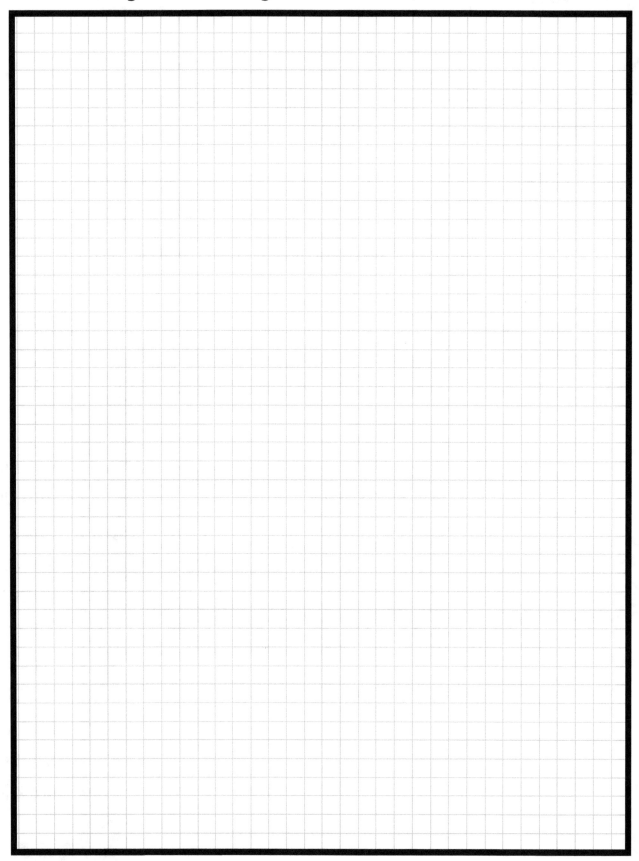

CIRCLE TODAY'S DATE

January
February
March
April
May
June
July
August
September
October
November
December

1 2 3 4 5 6
7 8 9 10 11
12 13 14 15
16 17 18 19
20 21 22 23
24 25 26 27
28 29 30 31

MONDAY
TUESDAY
WEDNESDAY
THURSDAY
FRIDAY
SATURDAY
SUNDAY

2018
2019
2020
2021
2022
2023
2024
2025
2026
2027
2028
2029
2030
2031

Write Today's Date:_ _ _ _ _ _ _ _ _ _ _ _ _ _

FEELINGS, PLANS & THOUGHTS

Copy a Quote or Verse:

_____

_____

_____

_____

_____

_____

Draw a picture about your feelings:

To-Do List

_____

_____

_____

_____

_____

_____

ALL ABOUT HORSES:

Choose a Horse Breed to Research:

_____

List Four Facts about this Breed:

1._____
_____
2._____
_____
3._____
_____
4._____
_____

DRAW THIS TYPE OF HORSE OR TAPE A PICTURE HERE:

FEELINGS, PLANS & THOUGHTS

Copy a Quote or Verse:

_____
_____
_____
_____
_____
_____

Draw a picture
about your feelings:

To-Do List

_____
_____
_____
_____
_____
_____

Picture Study

Look closely at this picture.

Think about the lines and shadows.

Practice working with your colored pencils.

Draw the Missing Spot

Use a variety of smooth black drawing pens,
with fine points, to complete the picture.

NATURE STUDY

Go outside and make a realistic drawing
of something you find in nature.

Reading Time - 1 Hour (Set a Timer)

Choose Four Books - Read from each book for 15 minutes.

Copy important words and pictures from your books:

Spelling Time

Find 20 Words with 5 letters each.
Look in your books for words.
Write the words here:

_____   _____

_____   _____

_____   _____

_____   _____

_____   _____

_____   _____

_____   _____

_____   _____

_____   _____

_____   _____

Notes:

Ideas:

Movie Time

Watch a Documentary, Educational Program, Movie, or Tutorial.

TITLE:

_____

What did you Learn:

_____
_____
_____

Draw a scene from the video:

Rating:
AWFUL
BAD
LAME
YUCKY
OKAY
NICE
GOOD
GREAT
SUPER
AMAZING

CIRCLE TODAY'S DATE

January
February
March
April
May
June
July
August
September
October
November
December

1 2 3 4 5 6
7 8 9 10 11
12 13 14 15
16 17 18 19
20 21 22 23
24 25 26 27
28 29 30 31

MONDAY
TUESDAY
WEDNESDAY
THURSDAY
FRIDAY
SATURDAY
SUNDAY

2018
2019
2020
2021
2022
2023
2024
2025
2026
2027
2028
2029
2030
2031

Write Today's Date:_____

FEELINGS, PLANS & THOUGHTS

Copy a Quote or Verse:

_____

_____

_____

_____

_____

_____

Draw a picture
about your feelings:

To-Do List

_____

_____

_____

_____

_____

_____

MATH & CREATIVITY

Use this page for math problems

or design something like a house, farm or stable!

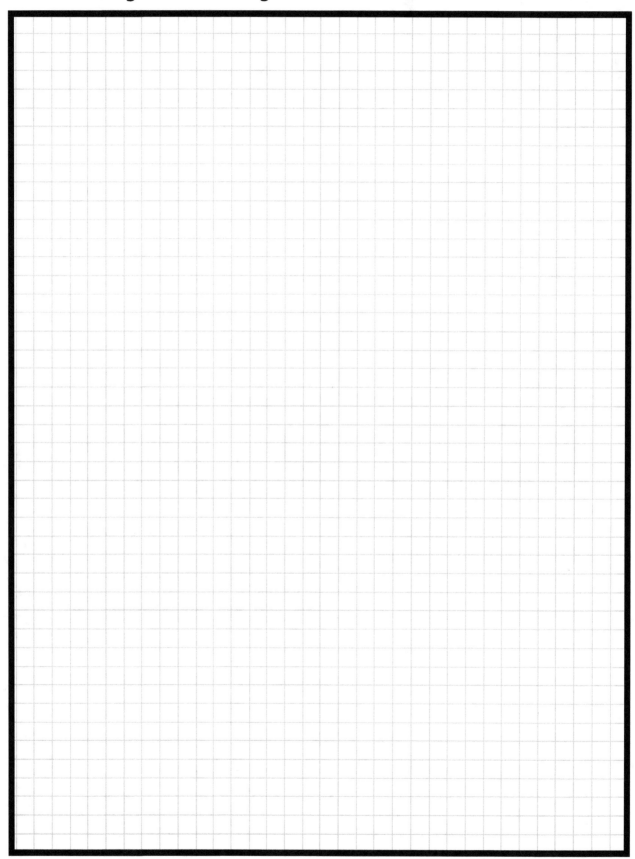

ALL ABOUT HORSES:

Choose a Horse Breed to Research:

_____

List Four Facts about this Breed:

1._____
_____
2._____
_____
3._____
_____
4._____
_____

DRAW THIS TYPE OF HORSE OR TAPE A PICTURE HERE:

Picture Study

Look closely at this picture.

Think about the lines and shadows.

Practice working with your colored pencils.

Draw the Missing Spot

Use a variety of smooth black drawing pens,
with fine points, to complete the picture.

NATURE STUDY

Go outside and make a realistic drawing
of something you find in nature.

Reading Time - 1 Hour (Set a Timer)

Choose Four Books - Read from each book for 15 minutes.

Copy important words and pictures from your books:

CIRCLE TODAY'S DATE

January
February
March
April
May
June
July
August
September
October
November
December

1 2 3 4 5 6
7 8 9 10 11
12 13 14 15
16 17 18 19
20 21 22 23
24 25 26 27
28 29 30 31

MONDAY
TUESDAY
WEDNESDAY
THURSDAY
FRIDAY
SATURDAY
SUNDAY

2018
2019
2020
2021
2022
2023
2024
2025
2026
2027
2028
2029
2030
2031

Write Today's Date: _ _ _ _ _ _ _ _ _ _ _ _ _ _

144

FEELINGS, PLANS & THOUGHTS

Copy a Quote or Verse:

_____
_____
_____
_____
_____
_____

Draw a picture about your feelings:

To-Do List

_____
_____
_____
_____
_____
_____

Spelling Time

Find 20 Words with **4** letters each.
Look in your books for words.
Write the words here:

_____	_____

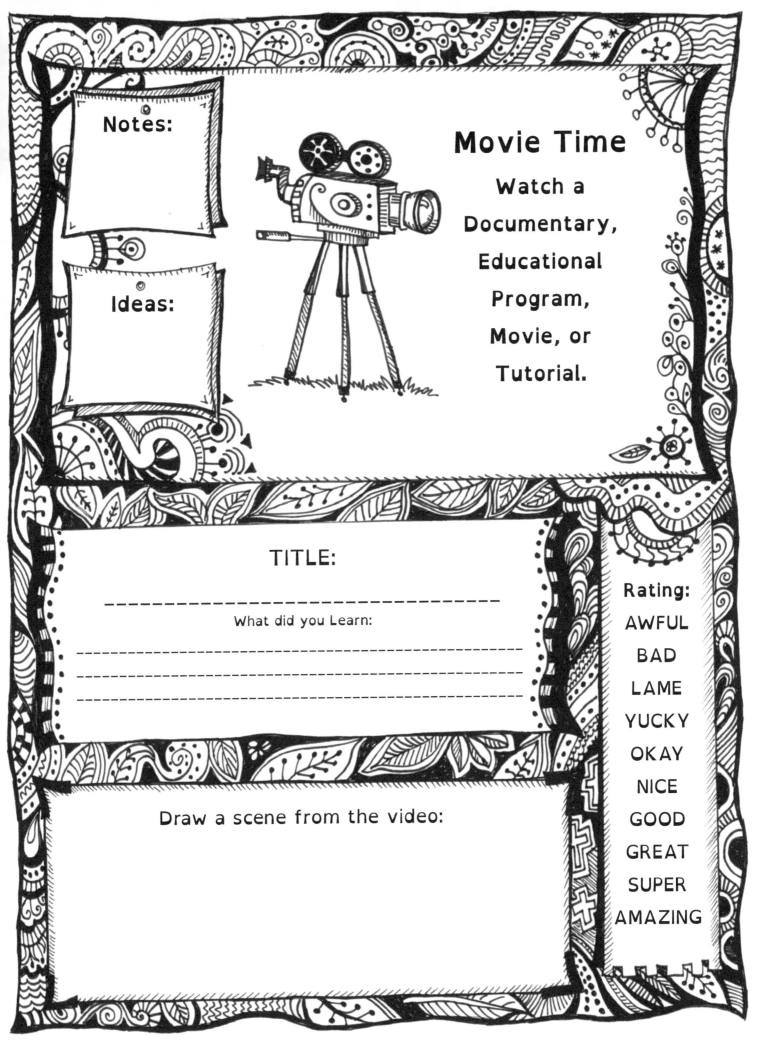

Notes:

Ideas:

Movie Time

Watch a Documentary, Educational Program, Movie, or Tutorial.

TITLE:

_____

What did you Learn:

_____
_____
_____

Draw a scene from the video:

Rating:
AWFUL
BAD
LAME
YUCKY
OKAY
NICE
GOOD
GREAT
SUPER
AMAZING

Listening Time

Listen to an audio book or classical music or
ask someone to read a story to you while
you color and draw on the next page.

What are you listening to?

_____

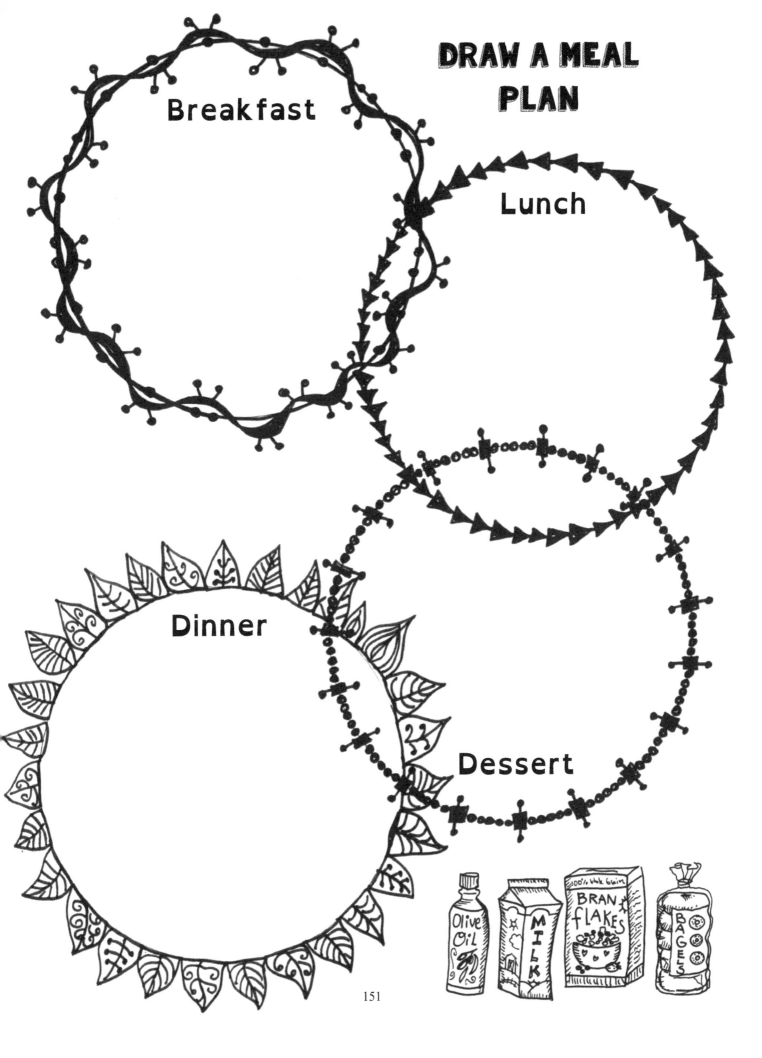

Breakfast

Lunch

DRAW A MEAL PLAN

Dinner

Dessert

151

Picture Study

Look closely at this picture.

Think about the lines and shadows.

Practice working with your colored pencils.

Draw the Missing Spot

Use a variety of smooth black drawing pens,
with fine points, to complete the picture.

CIRCLE TODAY'S DATE

January
February
March
April
May
June
July
August
September
October
November
December

1 2 3 4 5 6
7 8 9 10 11
12 13 14 15
16 17 18 19
20 21 22 23
24 25 26 27
28 29 30 31

MONDAY
TUESDAY
WEDNESDAY
THURSDAY
FRIDAY
SATURDAY
SUNDAY

2018
2019
2020
2021
2022
2023
2024
2025
2026
2027
2028
2029
2030
2031

Write Today's Date: _ _ _ _ _ _ _ _ _ _ _ _ _ _ _ _ _

FEELINGS, PLANS & THOUGHTS

Copy a Quote or Verse:

_____
_____
_____
_____
_____
_____

Draw a picture about your feelings:

To-Do List

_____
_____
_____
_____
_____
_____

NATURE STUDY

Go outside and make a realistic drawing
of something you find in nature.

Reading Time - 1 Hour (Set a Timer)

Choose Four Books - Read from each book for 15 minutes.

Copy important words and pictures from your books:

Spelling Time

Find 20 Words with **3** letters each.

Look in your books for words.

Write the words here:

_____	_____
_____	_____
_____	_____
_____	_____
_____	_____
_____	_____
_____	_____
_____	_____
_____	_____

Notes:

Ideas:

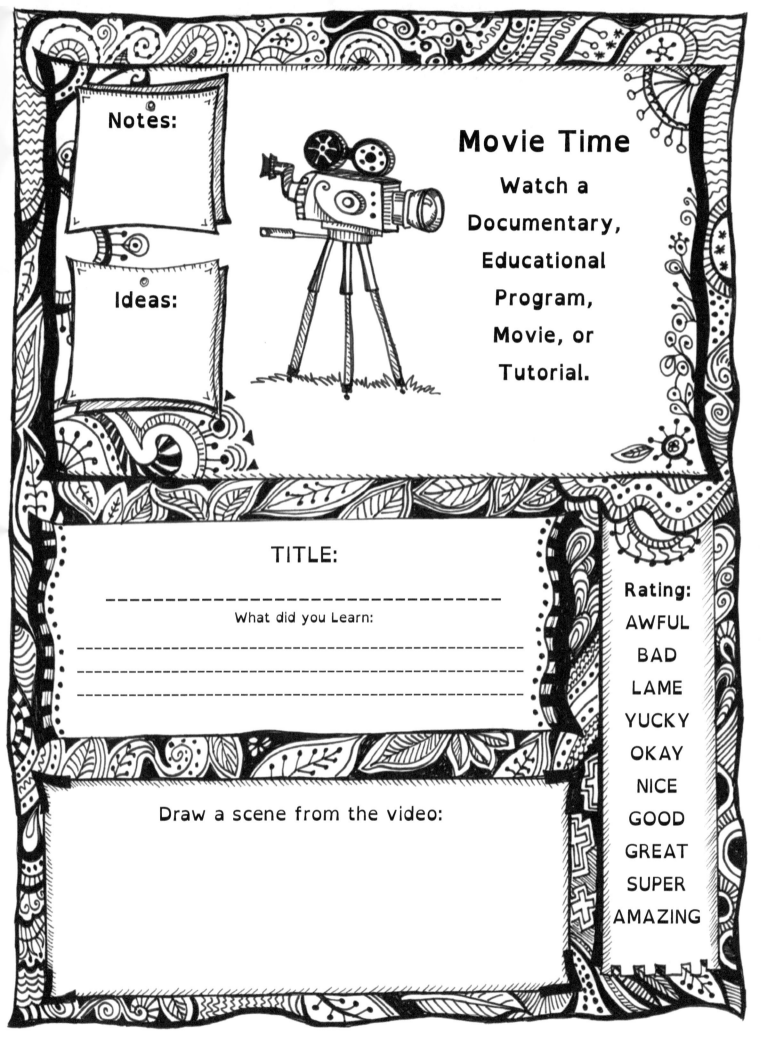

Movie Time

Watch a Documentary, Educational Program, Movie, or Tutorial.

TITLE:

_____

What did you Learn:

_____
_____
_____

Rating:

AWFUL

BAD

LAME

YUCKY

OKAY

NICE

GOOD

GREAT

SUPER

AMAZING

Draw a scene from the video:

MATH & CREATIVITY

Use this page for math problems
or design something like a house, farm or stable!

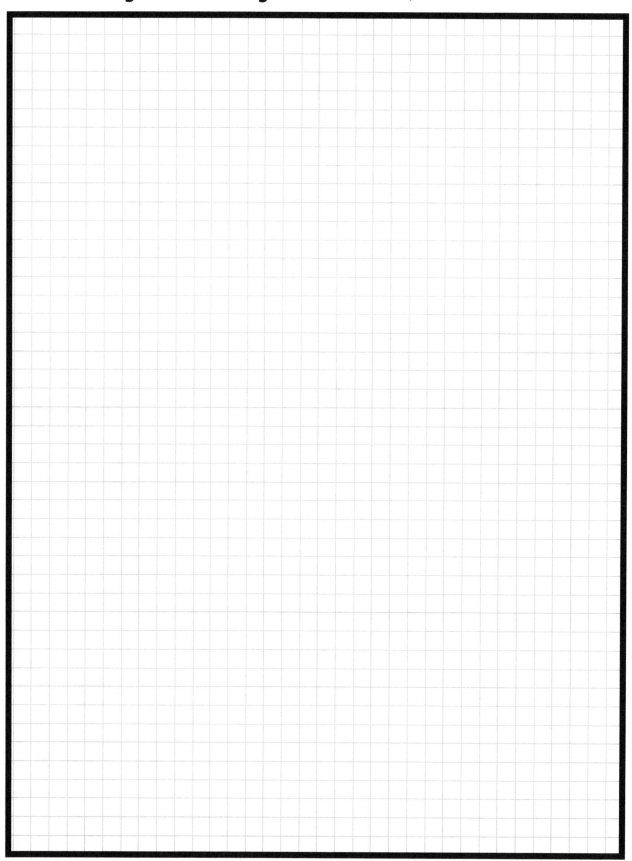

ALL ABOUT HORSES:

Choose a Horse Breed to Research:

_____

List Four Facts about this Breed:

1._____
_____

2._____
_____

3._____
_____

4._____
_____

DRAW THIS TYPE OF HORSE OR TAPE A PICTURE HERE:

My FUN Page

Picture Study

Look closely at this picture.

Think about the lines and shadows.

Practice working with your colored pencils.

Draw the Missing Spot

Use a variety of smooth black drawing pens,
with fine points, to complete the picture.

CIRCLE TODAY'S DATE

January
February
March
April
May
June
July
August
September
October
November
December

1 2 3 4 5 6
7 8 9 10 11
12 13 14 15
16 17 18 19
20 21 22 23
24 25 26 27
28 29 30 31

MONDAY
TUESDAY
WEDNESDAY
THURSDAY
FRIDAY
SATURDAY
SUNDAY

2018
2019
2020
2021
2022
2023
2024
2025
2026
2027
2028
2029
2030
2031

Write Today's Date: _ _ _ _ _ _ _ _ _ _ _ _ _ _

FEELINGS, PLANS & THOUGHTS

Copy a Quote or Verse:

_____
_____
_____
_____
_____
_____

Draw a picture about your feelings:

To-Do List

_____
_____
_____
_____
_____
_____

NATURE STUDY

Go outside and make a realistic drawing
of something you find in nature.

Reading Time - 1 Hour (Set a Timer)

Choose Four Books - Read from each book for 15 minutes.

Copy important words and pictures from your books:

Notes:

Ideas:

Movie Time

Watch a Documentary, Educational Program, Movie, or Tutorial.

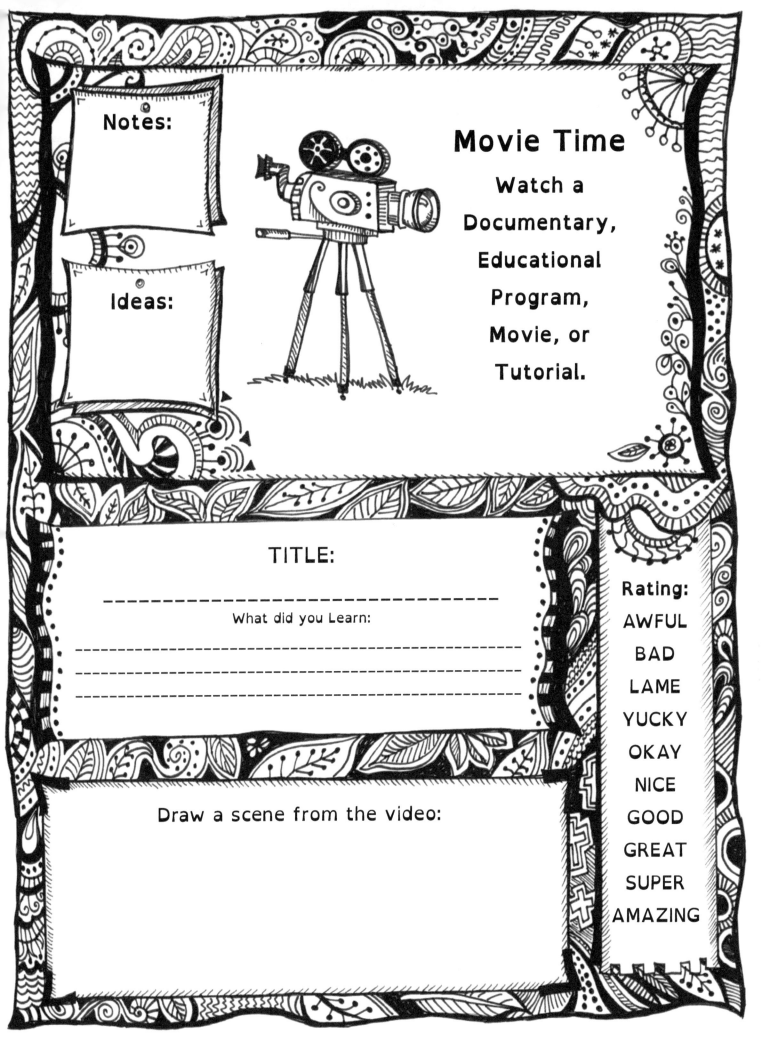

TITLE:

_____

What did you Learn:

_____
_____
_____

Rating:
AWFUL
BAD
LAME
YUCKY
OKAY
NICE
GOOD
GREAT
SUPER
AMAZING

Draw a scene from the video:

MATH & CREATIVITY

Use this page for math problems

or design something like a house, farm or stable!

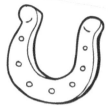

ALL ABOUT HORSES:

Choose a Horse Breed to Research:

_____

List Four Facts about this Breed:

1._____
_____

2._____
_____

3._____
_____

4._____
_____

DRAW THIS TYPE OF HORSE OR TAPE A PICTURE HERE:

Picture Study

Look closely at this picture.

Think about the lines and shadows.

Practice working with your colored pencils.

Draw the Missing Spot

Use a variety of smooth black drawing pens,
with fine points, to complete the picture.

CIRCLE TODAY'S DATE

January
February
March
April
May
June
July
August
September
October
November
December

1 2 3 4 5 6
7 8 9 10 11
12 13 14 15
16 17 18 19
20 21 22 23
24 25 26 27
28 29 30 31

MONDAY
TUESDAY
WEDNESDAY
THURSDAY
FRIDAY
SATURDAY
SUNDAY

2018
2019
2020
2021
2022
2023
2024
2025
2026
2027
2028
2029
2030
2031

Write Today's Date: _ _ _ _ _ _ _ _ _ _ _ _ _ _ _

FEELINGS, PLANS & THOUGHTS

Copy a Quote or Verse:

_____
_____
_____
_____
_____
_____

Draw a picture
about your feelings:

To-Do List

_____
_____
_____
_____
_____
_____

179

NATURE STUDY

Go outside and make a realistic drawing
of something you find in nature.

Reading Time - 1 Hour (Set a Timer)

Choose Four Books - Read from each book for 15 minutes.

Copy important words and pictures from your books:

Spelling Time

Find 20 Words with **5** letters each.

Look in your books for words.

Write the words here:

_____   _____

_____   _____

_____   _____

_____   _____

_____   _____

_____   _____

_____   _____

_____   _____

_____   _____

_____   _____

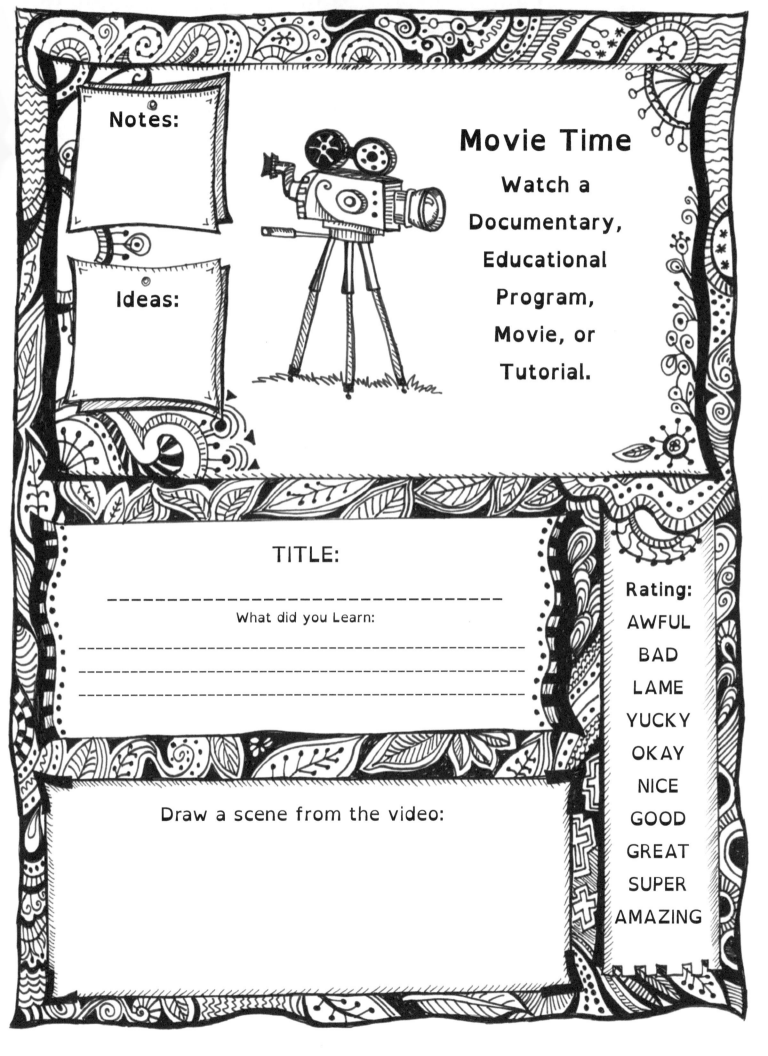

Notes:

Ideas:

Movie Time

Watch a Documentary, Educational Program, Movie, or Tutorial.

TITLE:

_____

What did you Learn:

_____
_____
_____

Draw a scene from the video:

Rating:

AWFUL

BAD

LAME

YUCKY

OKAY

NICE

GOOD

GREAT

SUPER

AMAZING

MATH & CREATIVITY

Use this page for math problems

or design something like a house, farm or stable!

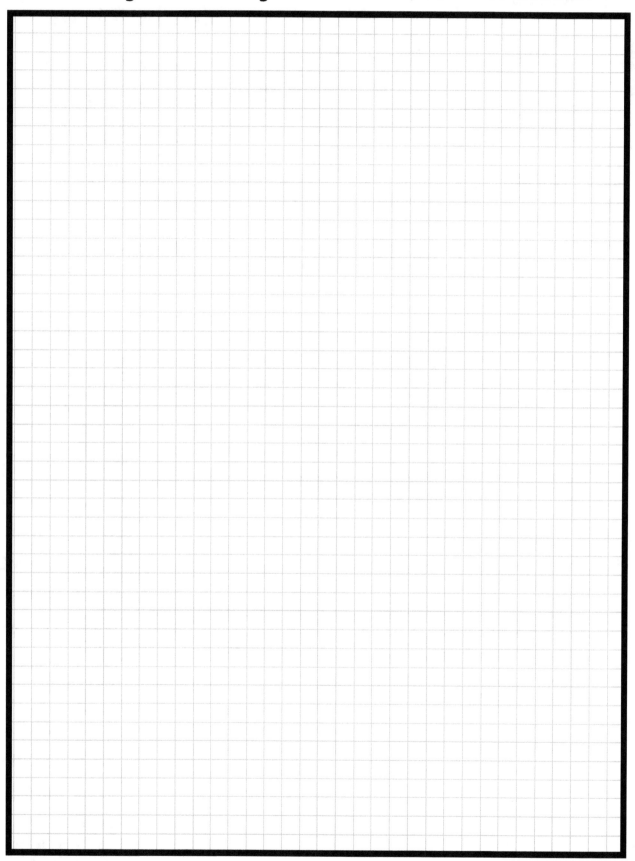

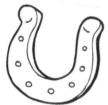

ALL ABOUT HORSES:

Choose a Horse Breed to Research:

_____

List Four Facts about this Breed:

1._____
_____
2._____
_____
3._____
_____
4._____
_____

DRAW THIS TYPE OF HORSE OR TAPE A PICTURE HERE:

World News Today!

Talk to your parents about current events.

Look at a newspaper, news broadcast or website.

Color the countries you learn about.

Tell the news stories with words or pictures.

CIRCLE TODAY'S DATE

January
February
March
April
May
June
July
August
September
October
November
December

1 2 3 4 5 6
7 8 9 10 11
12 13 14 15
16 17 18 19
20 21 22 23
24 25 26 27
28 29 30 31

MONDAY
TUESDAY
WEDNESDAY
THURSDAY
FRIDAY
SATURDAY
SUNDAY

2018
2019
2020
2021
2022
2023
2024
2025
2026
2027
2028
2029
2030
2031

Write Today's Date:_ _ _ _ _ _ _ _ _ _ _ _ _ _ _

FEELINGS, PLANS & THOUGHTS

Copy a Quote or Verse:

_____

_____

_____

_____

_____

_____

Draw a picture
about your feelings:

To-Do List

_____

_____

_____

_____

_____

_____

189

NATURE STUDY

Go outside and make a realistic drawing
of something you find in nature.

Reading Time - 1 Hour (Set a Timer)

Choose Four Books - Read from each book for 15 minutes.

Copy important words and pictures from your books:

Notes:

Ideas:

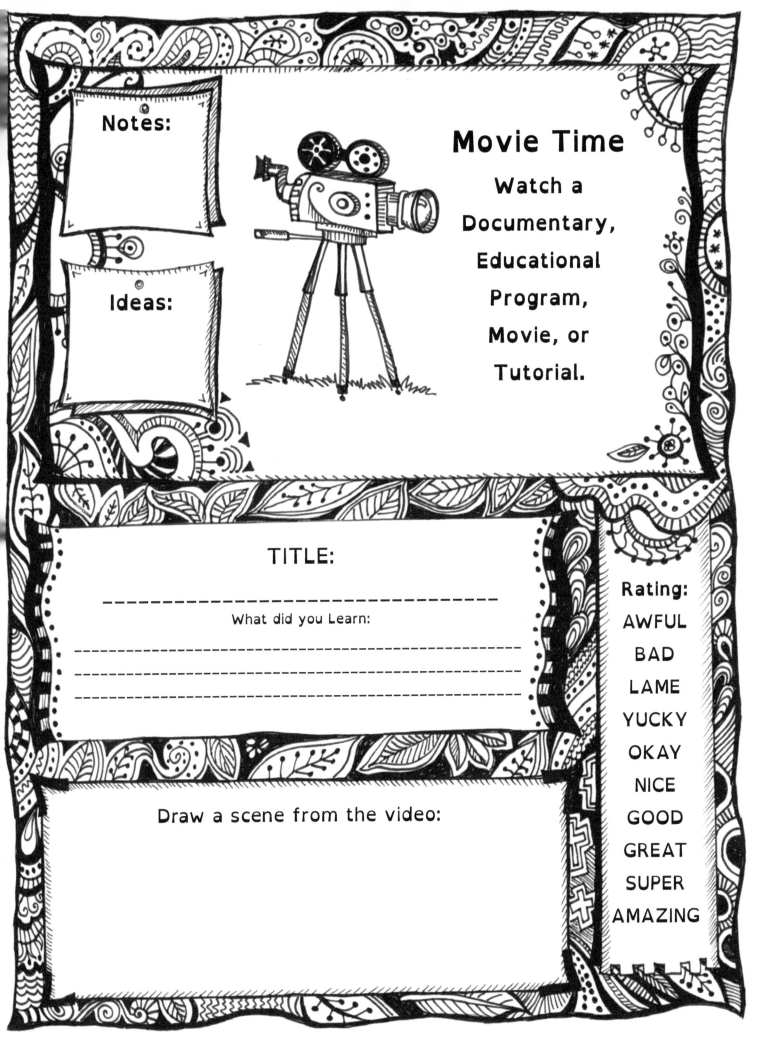

Movie Time

Watch a Documentary, Educational Program, Movie, or Tutorial.

TITLE:

_____

What did you Learn:

_____
_____
_____

Draw a scene from the video:

Rating:

AWFUL

BAD

LAME

YUCKY

OKAY

NICE

GOOD

GREAT

SUPER

AMAZING

MATH & CREATIVITY

Use this page for math problems
or design something like a house, farm or stable!

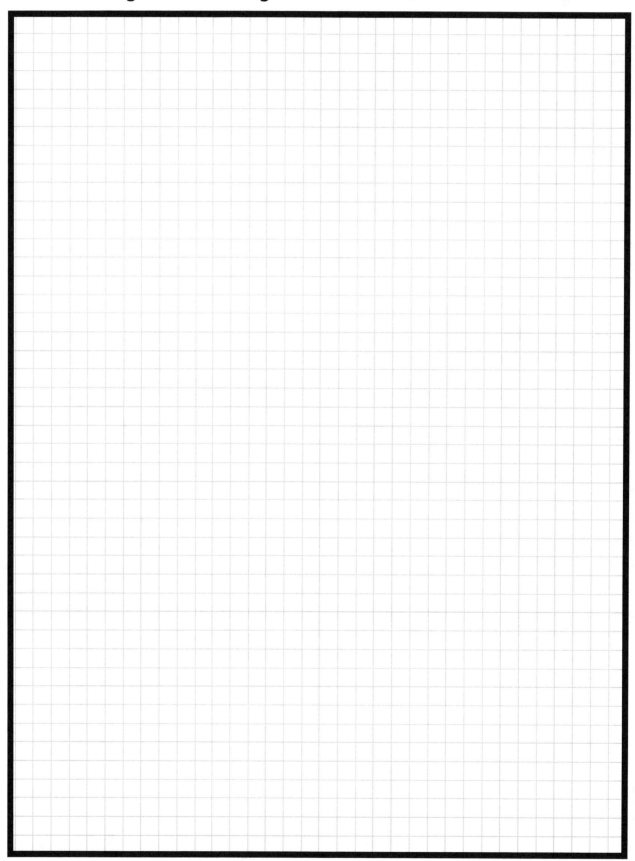

World News Today!

Talk to your parents about current events.

Look at a newspaper, news broadcast or website.

Color the countries you learn about.

Tell the news stories with words or pictures.

ALL ABOUT HORSES:

Choose a Horse Breed to Research:

_____

List Four Facts about this Breed:

1._____
_____
2._____
_____
3._____
_____
4._____
_____

DRAW THIS TYPE OF HORSE OR TAPE A PICTURE HERE:

Create a Comic Strip!

CIRCLE TODAY'S DATE

January
February
March
April
May
June
July
August
September
October
November
December

1 2 3 4 5 6
7 8 9 10 11
12 13 14 15
16 17 18 19
20 21 22 23
24 25 26 27
28 29 30 31

MONDAY
TUESDAY
WEDNESDAY
THURSDAY
FRIDAY
SATURDAY
SUNDAY

2018
2019
2020
2021
2022
2023
2024
2025
2026
2027
2028
2029
2030
2031

Write Today's Date: _ _ _ _ _ _ _ _ _ _ _ _ _ _ _

FEELINGS, PLANS & THOUGHTS

Copy a Quote or Verse:

_____
_____
_____
_____
_____
_____

Draw a picture about your feelings:

To-Do List

_____
_____
_____
_____
_____
_____

Picture Study

Look closely at this picture.

Think about the lines and shadows.

Practice working with your colored pencils.

Draw the Missing Spot

Use a variety of smooth black drawing pens,
with fine points, to complete the picture.

NATURE STUDY

Go outside and make a realistic drawing
of something you find in nature.

Reading Time - 1 Hour (Set a Timer)

Choose Four Books - Read from each book for 15 minutes.

Copy important words and pictures from your books:

Spelling Time

Find 20 Words with **7** letters each.

Look in your books for words.

Write the words here:

_____ _____

_____ _____

_____ _____

_____ _____

_____ _____

_____ _____

_____ _____

_____ _____

_____ _____

_____ _____

Notes:

Ideas:

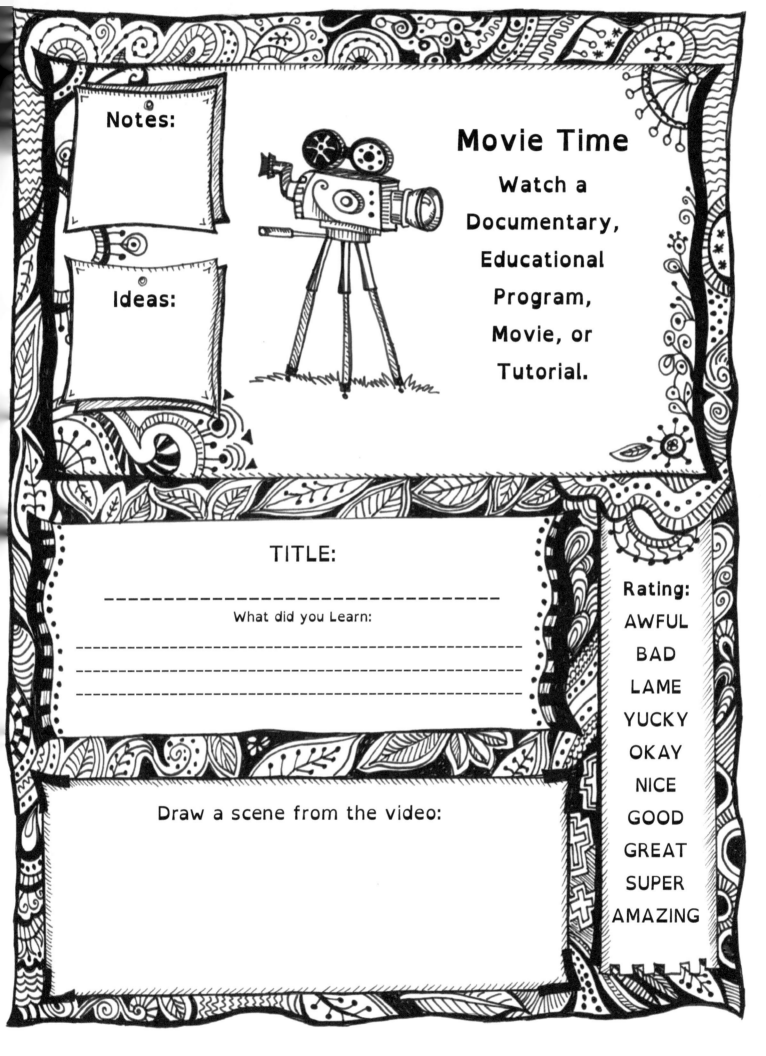

Movie Time

Watch a Documentary, Educational Program, Movie, or Tutorial.

TITLE:

_____

What did you Learn:

_____
_____
_____

Draw a scene from the video:

Rating:
AWFUL
BAD
LAME
YUCKY
OKAY
NICE
GOOD
GREAT
SUPER
AMAZING

MATH & CREATIVITY

Use this page for math problems
or design something like a house, farm or stable!

ALL ABOUT HORSES:

Choose a Horse Breed to Research:

_____

List Four Facts about this Breed:

1._____
_____
2._____
_____
3._____
_____
4._____
_____

DRAW THIS TYPE OF HORSE OR TAPE A PICTURE HERE:

CIRCLE TODAY'S DATE

January
February
March
April
May
June
July
August
September
October
November
December

1 2 3 4 5 6
7 8 9 10 11
12 13 14 15
16 17 18 19
20 21 22 23
24 25 26 27
28 29 30 31

MONDAY
TUESDAY
WEDNESDAY
THURSDAY
FRIDAY
SATURDAY
SUNDAY

2018
2019
2020
2021
2022
2023
2024
2025
2026
2027
2028
2029
2030
2031

Write Today's Date: _ _ _ _ _ _ _ _ _ _ _ _ _ _ _

My FUN Page

FEELINGS, PLANS & THOUGHTS

Copy a Quote or Verse:

_____

_____

_____

_____

_____

_____

Draw a picture about your feelings:

To-Do List

_____

_____

_____

_____

_____

_____

NATURE STUDY

Go outside and make a realistic drawing
of something you find in nature.

Reading Time - 1 Hour (Set a Timer)

Choose Four Books - Read from each book for 15 minutes.

Copy important words and pictures from your books:

Spelling Time

Find 20 Words with **8** letters each.
Look in your books for words.
Write the words here:

_____   _____

_____   _____

_____   _____

_____   _____

_____   _____

_____   _____

_____   _____

_____   _____

_____   _____

Notes:

Ideas:

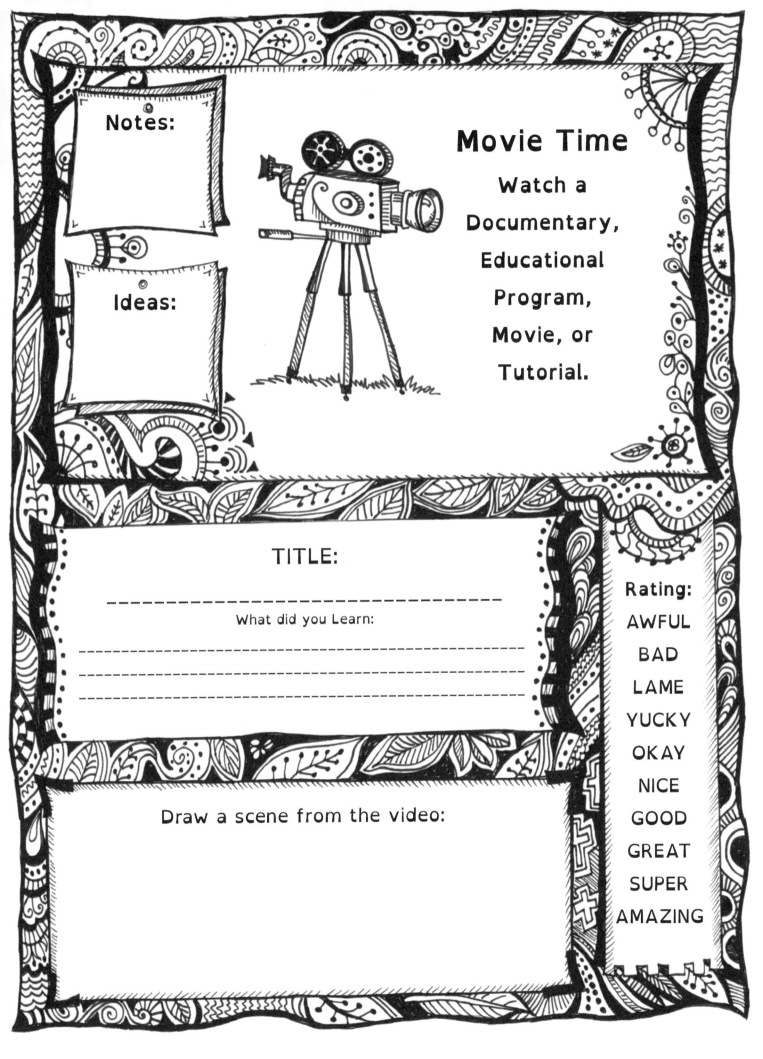

Movie Time

Watch a Documentary, Educational Program, Movie, or Tutorial.

TITLE:

_____

What did you Learn:

Draw a scene from the video:

Rating:

AWFUL

BAD

LAME

YUCKY

OKAY

NICE

GOOD

GREAT

SUPER

AMAZING

MATH & CREATIVITY

Use this page for math problems
or design something like a house, farm or stable!

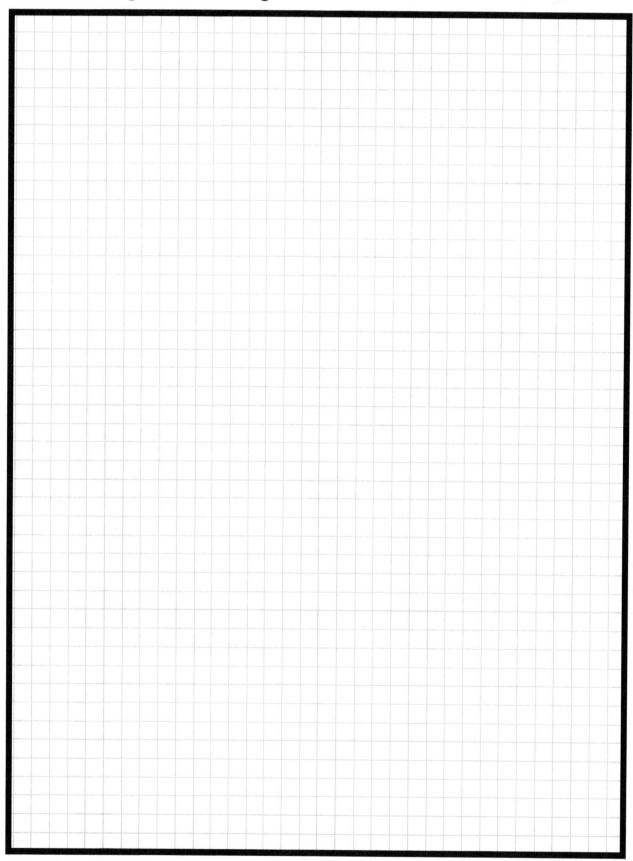

CIRCLE TODAY'S DATE

January
February
March
April
May
June
July
August
September
October
November
December

1 2 3 4 5 6
7 8 9 10 11
12 13 14 15
16 17 18 19
20 21 22 23
24 25 26 27
28 29 30 31

MONDAY
TUESDAY
WEDNESDAY
THURSDAY
FRIDAY
SATURDAY
SUNDAY

2018
2019
2020
2021
2022
2023
2024
2025
2026
2027
2028
2029
2030
2031

Write Today's Date: _ _ _ _ _ _ _ _ _ _ _ _ _ _

FEELINGS, PLANS & THOUGHTS

Copy a Quote or Verse:

_____

_____

_____

_____

_____

_____

Draw a picture
about your feelings:

To-Do List

_____

_____

_____

_____

_____

_____

Picture Study

Look closely at this picture.

Think about the lines and shadows.

Practice working with your colored pencils.

Reading Time - 1 Hour (Set a Timer)

Choose Four Books - Read from each book for 15 minutes.

Copy important words and pictures from your books:

Spelling Time

Find 20 Words with **9** letters each.

Look in your books for words.

Write the words here:

Notes:

Ideas:

Movie Time

Watch a Documentary, Educational Program, Movie, or Tutorial.

TITLE:

_____

What did you Learn:

_____
_____
_____

Draw a scene from the video:

Rating:
AWFUL
BAD
LAME
YUCKY
OKAY
NICE
GOOD
GREAT
SUPER
AMAZING

CIRCLE TODAY'S DATE

January
February
March
April
May
June
July
August
September
October
November
December

1 2 3 4 5 6
7 8 9 10 11
12 13 14 15
16 17 18 19
20 21 22 23
24 25 26 27
28 29 30 31

MONDAY
TUESDAY
WEDNESDAY
THURSDAY
FRIDAY
SATURDAY
SUNDAY

2018
2019
2020
2021
2022
2023
2024
2025
2026
2027
2028
2029
2030
2031

Write Today's Date: _ _ _ _ _ _ _ _ _ _ _ _ _ _

FEELINGS, PLANS & THOUGHTS

Copy a Quote or Verse:

Draw a picture about your feelings:

To-Do List

_____

_____

_____

_____

_____

_____

MATH & CREATIVITY

Use this page for math problems

or design something like a house, farm or stable!

World News Today!

Talk to your parents about current events.

Look at a newspaper, news broadcast or website.

Color the countries you learn about.

Tell the news stories with words or pictures.

ALL ABOUT HORSES:

Choose a Horse Breed to Research:

_____

List Four Facts about this Breed:

1._____
_____
2._____
_____
3._____
_____
4._____
_____

DRAW THIS TYPE OF HORSE OR TAPE A PICTURE HERE:

Create a Comic Strip!

Picture Study

Look closely at this picture.

Think about the lines and shadows.

Practice working with your colored pencils.

Draw the Missing Spot

Use a variety of smooth black drawing pens,
with fine points, to complete the picture.

NATURE STUDY

Go outside and make a realistic drawing
of something you find in nature.

Reading Time - 1 Hour (Set a Timer)

Choose Four Books - Read from each book for 15 minutes.

Copy important words and pictures from your books:

Spelling Time

Find 20 Words with **8** letters each.

Look in your books for words.

Write the words here:

_____   _____

_____   _____

_____   _____

_____   _____

_____   _____

_____   _____

_____   _____

_____   _____

_____   _____

_____   _____

CIRCLE TODAY'S DATE

January
February
March
April
May
June
July
August
September
October
November
December

1 2 3 4 5 6
7 8 9 10 11
12 13 14 15
16 17 18 19
20 21 22 23
24 25 26 27
28 29 30 31

MONDAY
TUESDAY
WEDNESDAY
THURSDAY
FRIDAY
SATURDAY
SUNDAY

2018
2019
2020
2021
2022
2023
2024
2025
2026
2027
2028
2029
2030
2031

Write Today's Date: _ _ _ _ _ _ _ _ _ _ _ _ _ _ _

FEELINGS, PLANS & THOUGHTS

Copy a Quote or Verse:

_____

_____

_____

_____

_____

_____

Draw a picture
about your feelings:

To-Do List

_____

_____

_____

_____

_____

_____

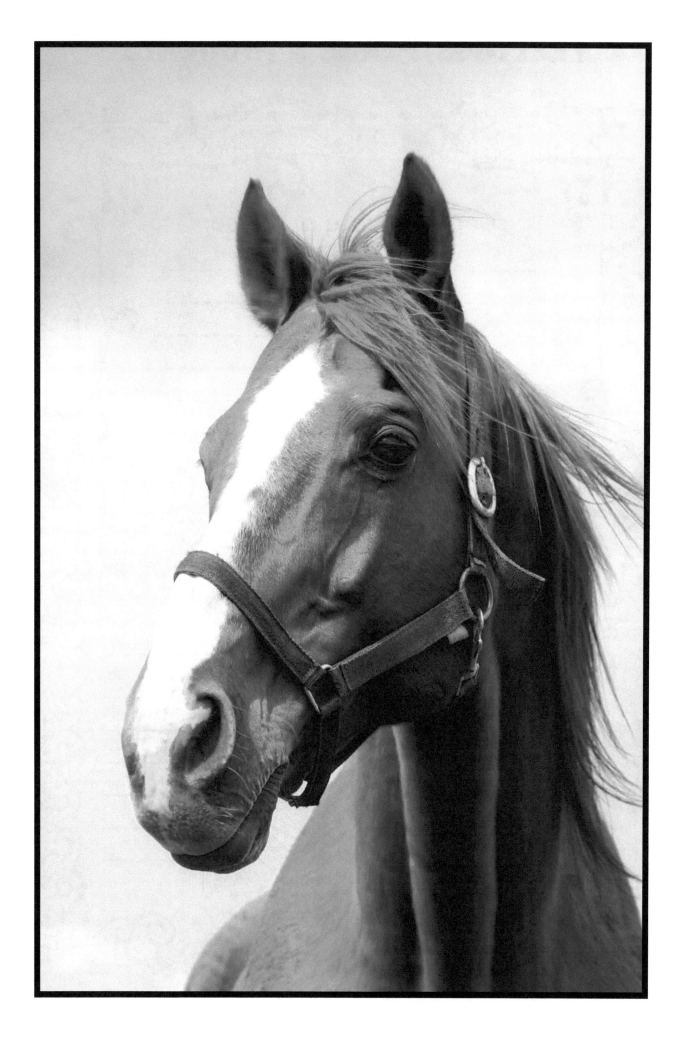

Notes:

Ideas:

Movie Time

Watch a Documentary, Educational Program, Movie, or Tutorial.

TITLE:

_____

What did you Learn:

_____
_____
_____

Draw a scene from the video:

Rating:
AWFUL
BAD
LAME
YUCKY
OKAY
NICE
GOOD
GREAT
SUPER
AMAZING

MATH & CREATIVITY

Use this page for math problems
or design something like a house, farm or stable!

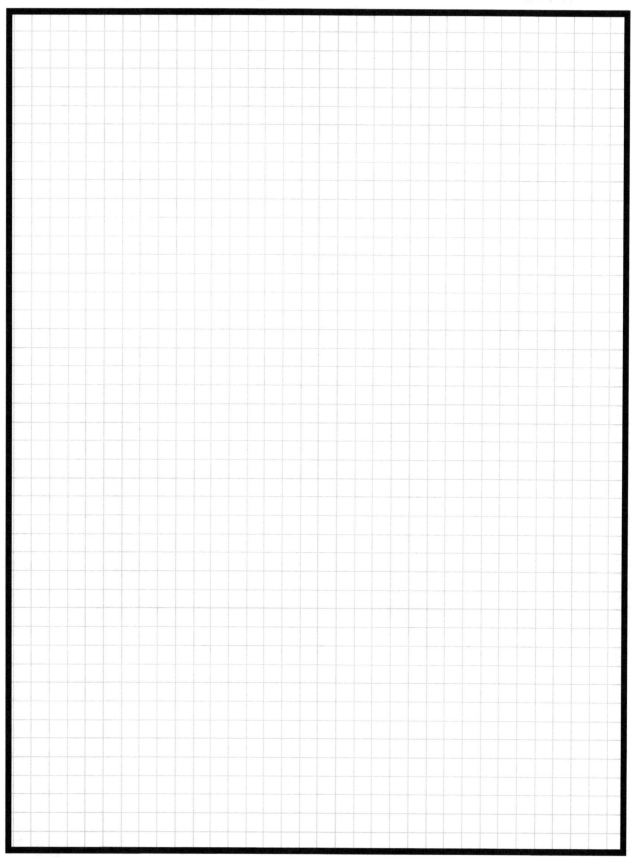

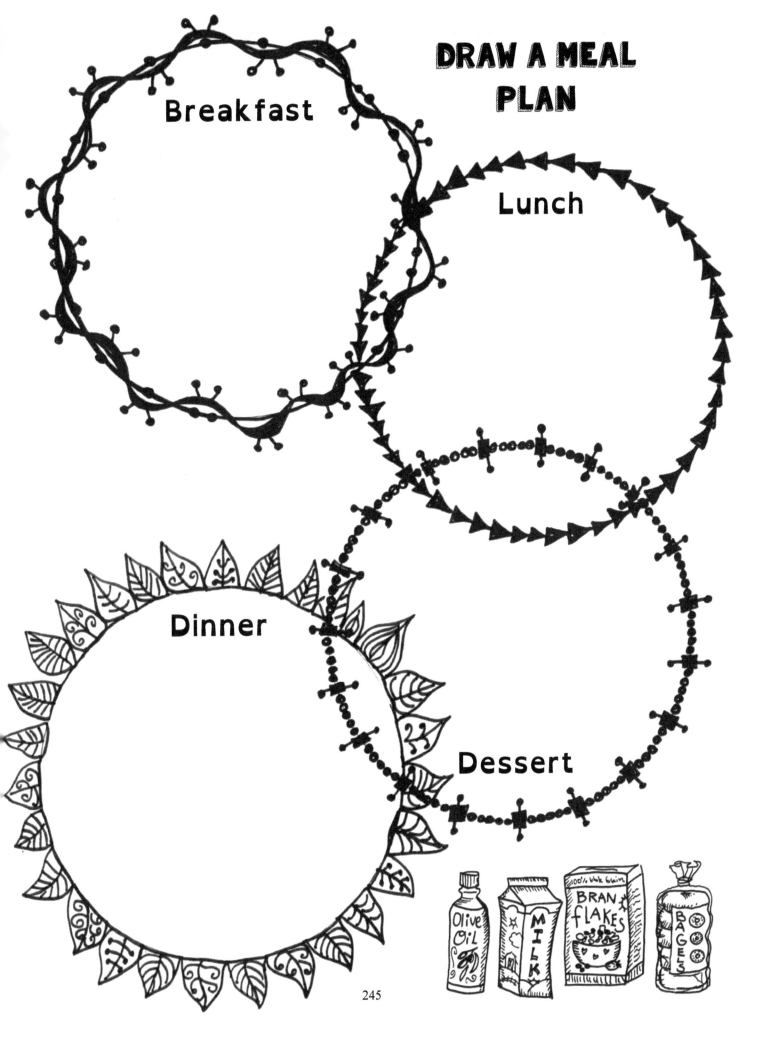

DRAW A MEAL PLAN

Breakfast

Lunch

Dinner

Dessert

245

ALL ABOUT HORSES:

Choose a Horse Breed to Research:

_____

List Four Facts about this Breed:

1._____
_____
2._____
_____
3._____
_____
4._____
_____

DRAW THIS TYPE OF HORSE OR TAPE A PICTURE HERE:

Create a Comic Strip!

NATURE STUDY

Go outside and make a realistic drawing
of something you find in nature.

Reading Time - 1 Hour (Set a Timer)

Choose Four Books - Read from each book for 15 minutes.
Copy important words and pictures from your books:

CIRCLE TODAY'S DATE

January
February
March
April
May
June
July
August
September
October
November
December

1 2 3 4 5 6
7 8 9 10 11
12 13 14 15
16 17 18 19
20 21 22 23
24 25 26 27
28 29 30 31

MONDAY
TUESDAY
WEDNESDAY
THURSDAY
FRIDAY
SATURDAY
SUNDAY

2018
2019
2020
2021
2022
2023
2024
2025
2026
2027
2028
2029
2030
2031

Write Today's Date:_ _ _ _ _ _ _ _ _ _ _ _ _

FEELINGS, PLANS & THOUGHTS

Copy a Quote or Verse:

_____

_____

_____

_____

_____

_____

Draw a picture
about your feelings:

To-Do List

_____

_____

_____

_____

_____

_____

Spelling Time

Find 20 Words with **8** letters each.

Look in your books for words.

Write the words here:

_____   _____

_____   _____

_____   _____

_____   _____

_____   _____

_____   _____

_____   _____

_____   _____

_____   _____

_____   _____

Notes:

Ideas:

Movie Time

Watch a Documentary, Educational Program, Movie, or Tutorial.

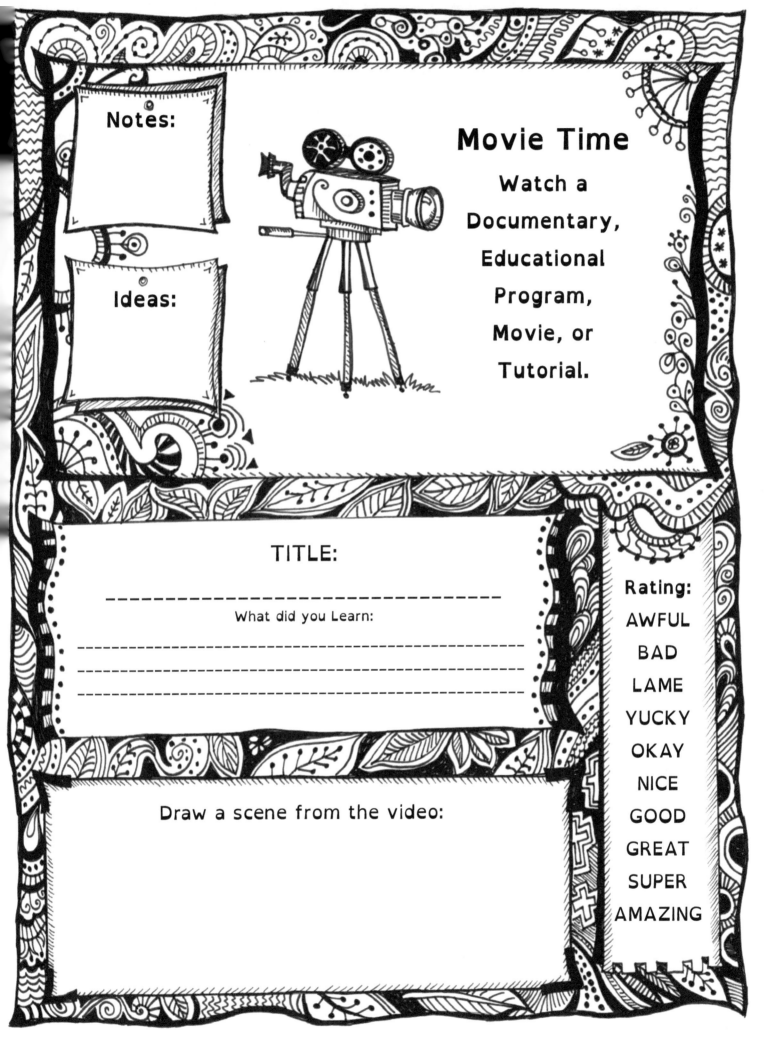

TITLE:

_____

What did you Learn:

_____

_____

_____

Draw a scene from the video:

Rating:

AWFUL

BAD

LAME

YUCKY

OKAY

NICE

GOOD

GREAT

SUPER

AMAZING

MATH & CREATIVITY

Use this page for math problems
or design something like a house, farm or stable!

ALL ABOUT HORSES:

Choose a Horse Breed to Research:

_____

List Four Facts about this Breed:

1._____
_____
2._____
_____
3._____
_____
4._____
_____

DRAW THIS TYPE OF HORSE OR TAPE A PICTURE HERE:

Create a Comic Strip!

ALL ABOUT HORSES:

Choose a Horse Breed to Research:

_____

List Four Facts about this Breed:

1._____
_____
2._____
_____
3._____
_____
4._____
_____

DRAW THIS TYPE OF HORSE OR TAPE A PICTURE HERE:

CIRCLE TODAY'S DATE

January
February
March
April
May
June
July
August
September
October
November
December

1 2 3 4 5 6
7 8 9 10 11
12 13 14 15
16 17 18 19
20 21 22 23
24 25 26 27
28 29 30 31

MONDAY
TUESDAY
WEDNESDAY
THURSDAY
FRIDAY
SATURDAY
SUNDAY

2018
2019
2020
2021
2022
2023
2024
2025
2026
2027
2028
2029
2030
2031

Write Today's Date: _ _ _ _ _ _ _ _ _ _ _ _ _ _ _

FEELINGS, PLANS & THOUGHTS

Copy a Quote or Verse:

_____

_____

_____

_____

_____

_____

Draw a picture
about your feelings:

To-Do List

_____

_____

_____

_____

_____

_____

My FUN Page

FEELINGS, PLANS & THOUGHTS

Copy a Quote or Verse:

_____

_____

_____

_____

_____

_____

Draw a picture
about your feelings:

To-Do List

_____

_____

_____

_____

_____

_____

Picture Study

Look closely at this picture.

Think about the lines and shadows.

Practice working with your colored pencils.

Draw the Missing Spot

Use a variety of smooth black drawing pens,
with fine points, to complete the picture.

NATURE STUDY

Go outside and make a realistic drawing
of something you find in nature.

Reading Time - 1 Hour (Set a Timer)

Choose Four Books - Read from each book for 15 minutes.

Copy important words and pictures from your books:

Spelling Time

Find 20 Words with 7 letters each.
Look in your books for words.
Write the words here:

_____ _____

_____ _____

_____ _____

_____ _____

_____ _____

_____ _____

_____ _____

_____ _____

_____ _____

_____ _____

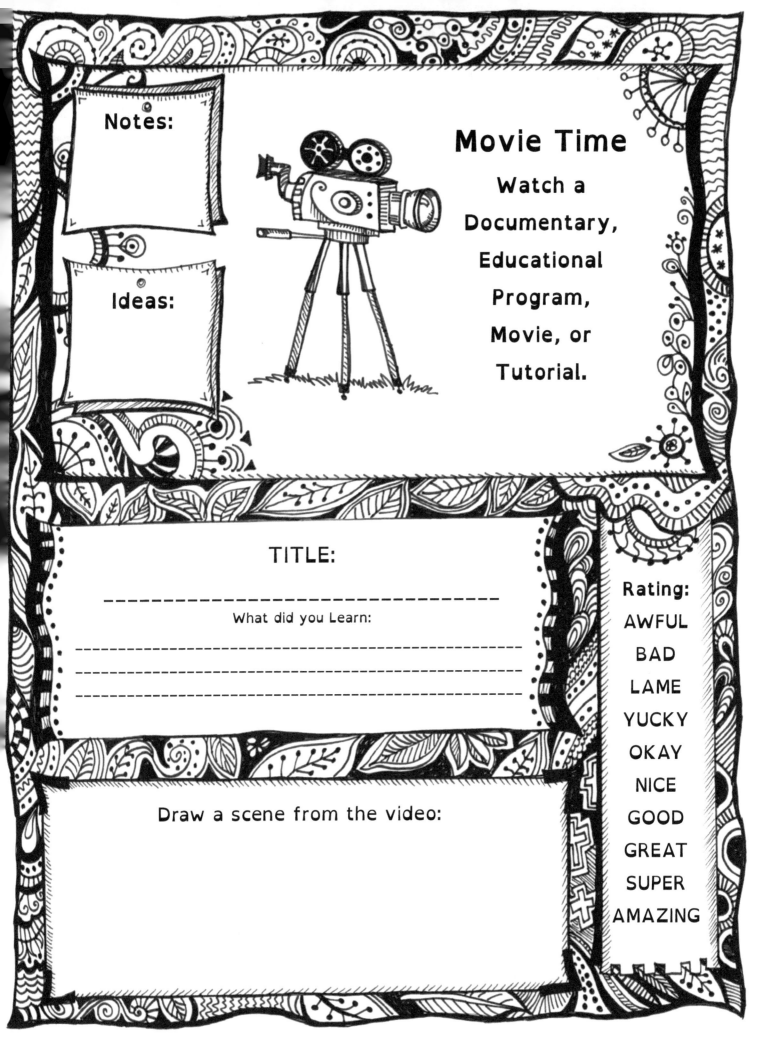

Notes:

Ideas:

Movie Time

Watch a Documentary, Educational Program, Movie, or Tutorial.

TITLE:

_____

What did you Learn:

Rating:

AWFUL

BAD

LAME

YUCKY

OKAY

NICE

GOOD

GREAT

SUPER

AMAZING

Draw a scene from the video:

MATH & CREATIVITY

Use this page for math problems
or design something like a house, farm or stable!

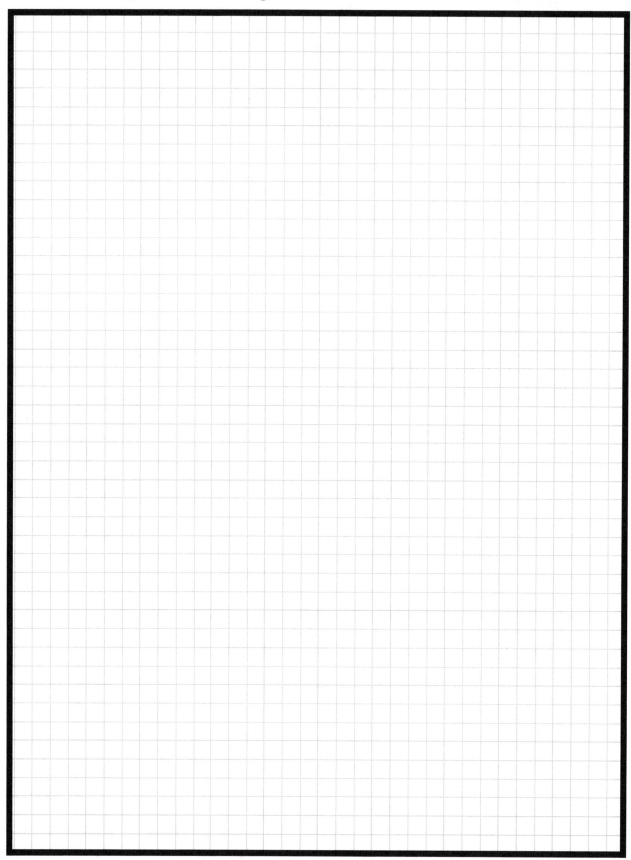

Fun Writing Practice:

ABCDEFGHIJKLMNOPQURSTUVWXYZ

abcdefghijklmnopqrstuvwxyz

ABCDEFGHIJKLMNOPQURSTUVWXYZ

ABCDEFGHIJKLMNOPQURSTUVWXYZ

abcdefghijklmnopqrstuvwxyz

CIRCLE TODAY'S DATE

January
February
March
April
May
June
July
August
September
October
November
December

1 2 3 4 5 6
7 8 9 10 11
12 13 14 15
16 17 18 19
20 21 22 23
24 25 26 27
28 29 30 31

MONDAY
TUESDAY
WEDNESDAY
THURSDAY
FRIDAY
SATURDAY
SUNDAY

2018
2019
2020
2021
2022
2023
2024
2025
2026
2027
2028
2029
2030
2031

Write Today's Date: _ _ _ _ _ _ _ _ _ _ _ _ _ _ _ _ _ _ _

FEELINGS, PLANS & THOUGHTS

Copy a Quote or Verse:

_____

_____

_____

_____

_____

_____

Draw a picture about your feelings:

To-Do List

ALL ABOUT HORSES:

Choose a Horse Breed to Research:

_____

List Four Facts about this Breed:

1._____
_____
2._____
_____
3._____
_____
4._____
_____

DRAW THIS TYPE OF HORSE OR TAPE A PICTURE HERE:

Create a Comic Strip!

NATURE STUDY

Go outside and make a realistic drawing
of something you find in nature.

Reading Time - 1 Hour (Set a Timer)

Choose Four Books - Read from each book for 15 minutes.

Copy important words and pictures from your books:

Spelling Time

Find 20 Words with **6** letters each.
Look in your books for words.
Write the words here:

_____   _____

_____   _____

_____   _____

_____   _____

_____   _____

_____   _____

_____   _____

_____   _____

_____   _____

_____   _____

Notes:

Ideas:

Movie Time

Watch a Documentary, Educational Program, Movie, or Tutorial.

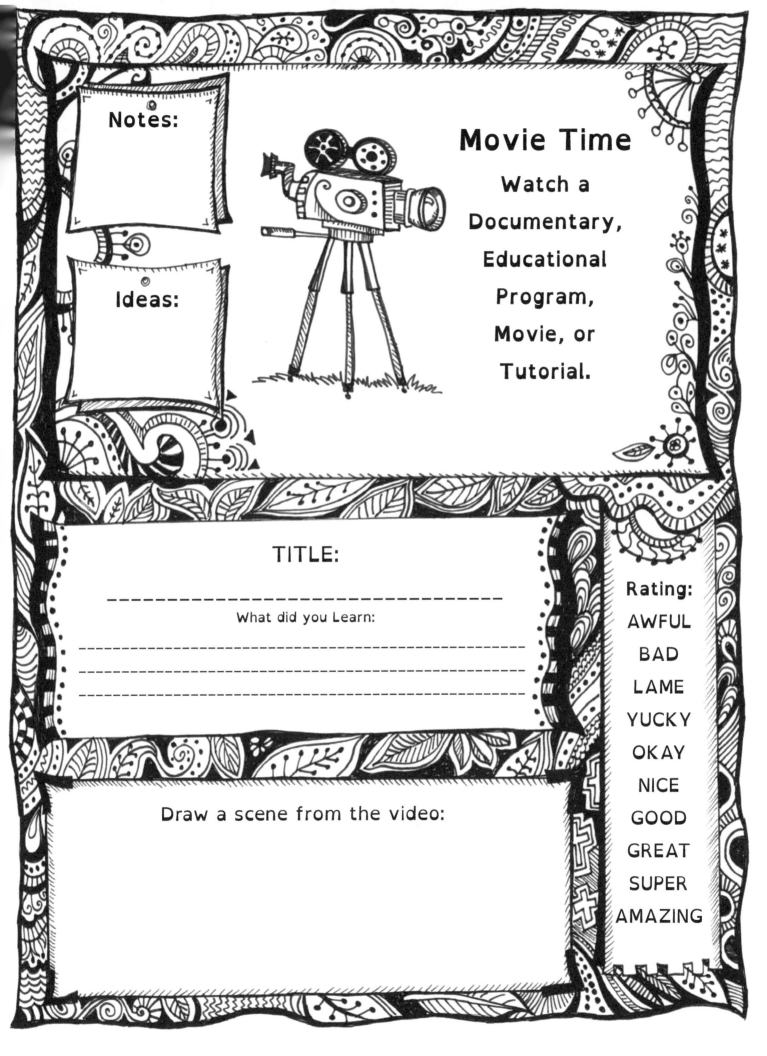

TITLE:

_____

What did you Learn:

_____
_____
_____

Draw a scene from the video:

Rating:

AWFUL

BAD

LAME

YUCKY

OKAY

NICE

GOOD

GREAT

SUPER

AMAZING

CIRCLE TODAY'S DATE

January
February
March
April
May
June
July
August
September
October
November
December

1 2 3 4 5 6
7 8 9 10 11
12 13 14 15
16 17 18 19
20 21 22 23
24 25 26 27
28 29 30 31

MONDAY
TUESDAY
WEDNESDAY
THURSDAY
FRIDAY
SATURDAY
SUNDAY

2018
2019
2020
2021
2022
2023
2024
2025
2026
2027
2028
2029
2030
2031

Write Today's Date: _ _ _ _ _ _ _ _ _ _ _ _ _ _ _

FEELINGS, PLANS & THOUGHTS

Copy a Quote or Verse:

_____
_____
_____
_____
_____
_____

Draw a picture about your feelings:

To-Do List

_____
_____
_____
_____
_____
_____

MATH & CREATIVITY

Use this page for math problems
or design something like a house, farm or stable!

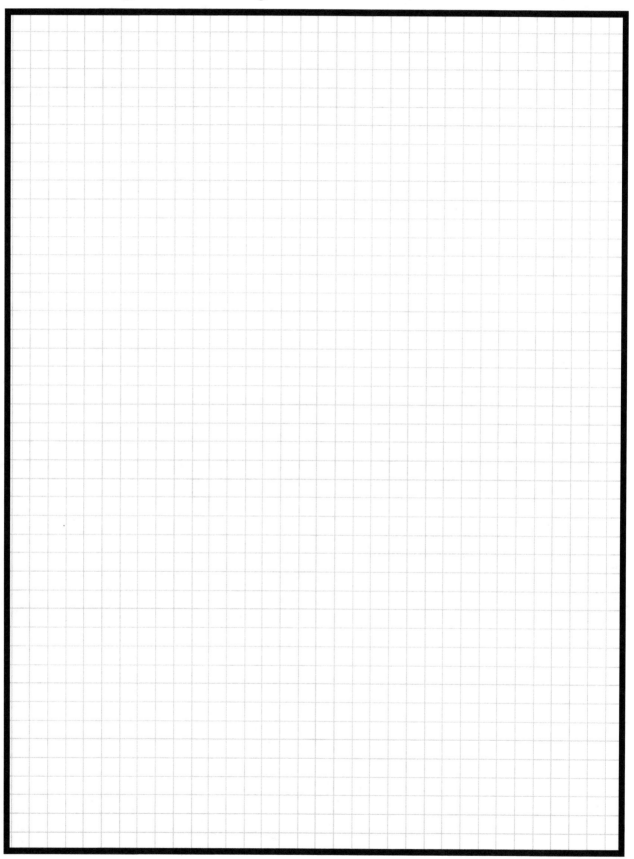

ALL ABOUT HORSES:

Choose a Horse Breed to Research:

_____

List Four Facts about this Breed:

1._____
_____
2._____
_____
3._____
_____
4._____
_____

DRAW THIS TYPE OF HORSE OR TAPE A PICTURE HERE:

Picture Study

Look closely at this picture.

Think about the lines and shadows.

Practice working with your colored pencils.

Draw the Missing Spot

Use a variety of smooth black drawing pens,
with fine points, to complete the picture.

NATURE STUDY

Go outside and make a realistic drawing
of something you find in nature.

288

Reading Time - 1 Hour (Set a Timer)

Choose Four Books - Read from each book for 15 minutes.

Copy important words and pictures from your books:

Spelling Time

Find 20 Words with 5 letters each.
Look in your books for words.
Write the words here:

_____   _____

_____   _____

_____   _____

_____   _____

_____   _____

_____   _____

_____   _____

_____   _____

_____   _____

_____   _____

Notes:

Ideas:

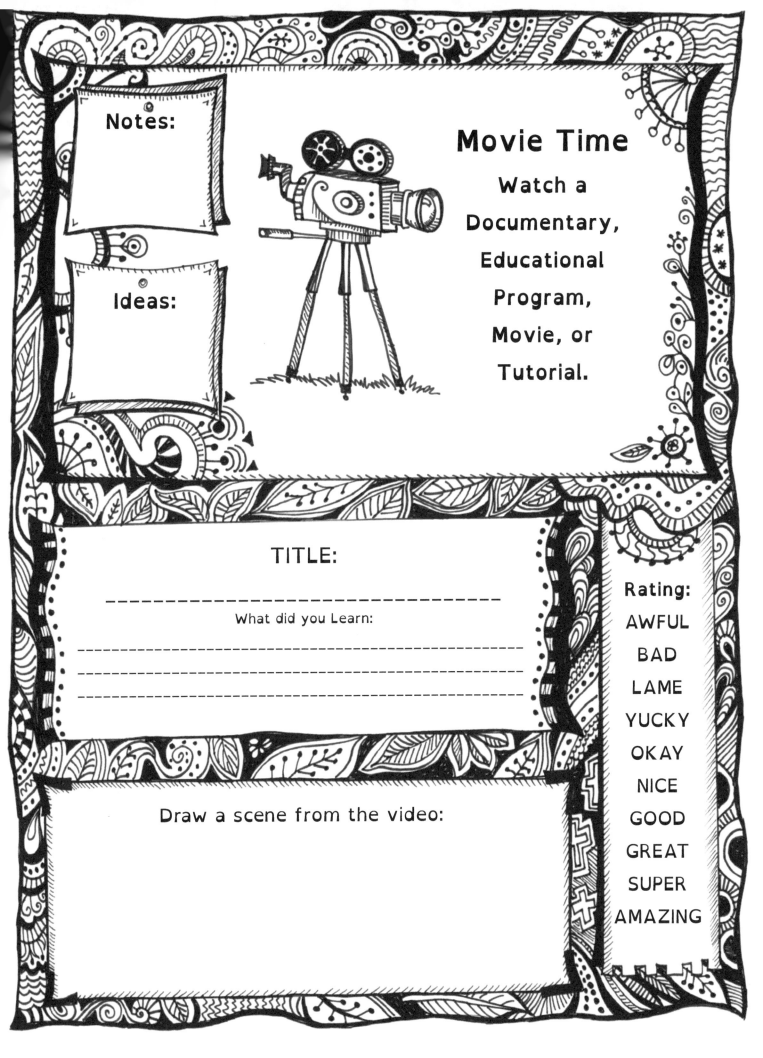

Movie Time

Watch a Documentary, Educational Program, Movie, or Tutorial.

TITLE:

_____

What did you Learn:

_____
_____
_____

Rating:
AWFUL
BAD
LAME
YUCKY
OKAY
NICE
GOOD
GREAT
SUPER
AMAZING

Draw a scene from the video:

CIRCLE TODAY'S DATE

January
February
March
April
May
June
July
August
September
October
November
December

1 2 3 4 5 6
7 8 9 10 11
12 13 14 15
16 17 18 19
20 21 22 23
24 25 26 27
28 29 30 31

MONDAY
TUESDAY
WEDNESDAY
THURSDAY
FRIDAY
SATURDAY
SUNDAY

2018
2019
2020
2021
2022
2023
2024
2025
2026
2027
2028
2029
2030
2031

Write Today's Date: _ _ _ _ _ _ _ _ _ _ _ _ _ _

FEELINGS, PLANS & THOUGHTS

Copy a Quote or Verse:

_____

_____

_____

_____

_____

_____

Draw a picture about your feelings:

To-Do List

_____

_____

_____

_____

_____

_____

MATH & CREATIVITY

Use this page for math problems
or design something like a house, farm or stable!

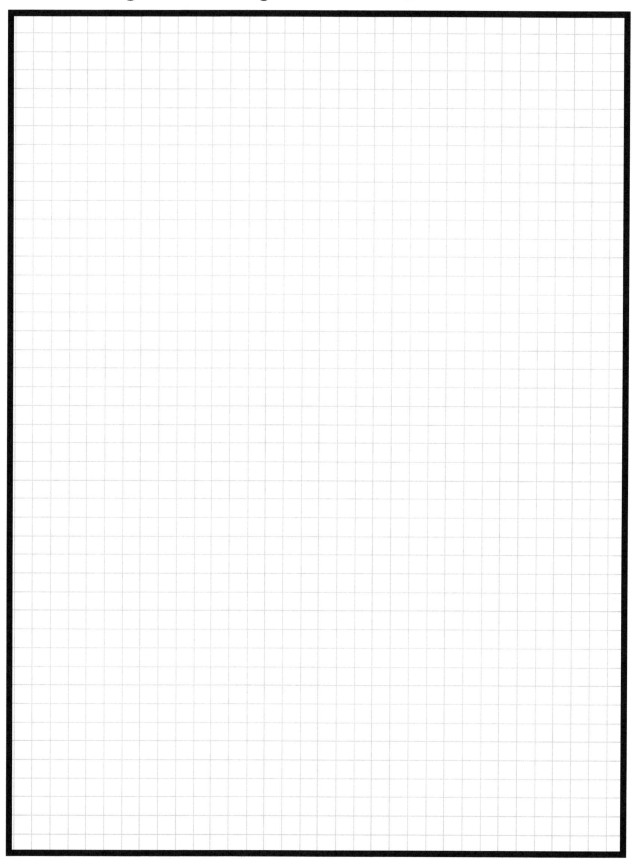

World News Today!

Talk to your parents about current events.

Look at a newspaper, news broadcast or website.

Color the countries you learn about.

Tell the news stories with words or pictures.

_____

_____

ALL ABOUT HORSES:

Choose a Horse Breed to Research:

_____

List Four Facts about this Breed:

1._____
_____
2._____
_____
3._____
_____
4._____
_____

DRAW THIS TYPE OF HORSE OR TAPE A PICTURE HERE:

NATURE STUDY

Go outside and make a realistic drawing
of something you find in nature.

Reading Time - 1 Hour (Set a Timer)

Choose Four Books - Read from each book for 15 minutes.

Copy important words and pictures from your books:

Spelling Time

Find 20 Words with 6 letters each.
Look in your books for words.
Write the words here:

_____   _____

_____   _____

_____   _____

_____   _____

_____   _____

_____   _____

_____   _____

_____   _____

_____   _____

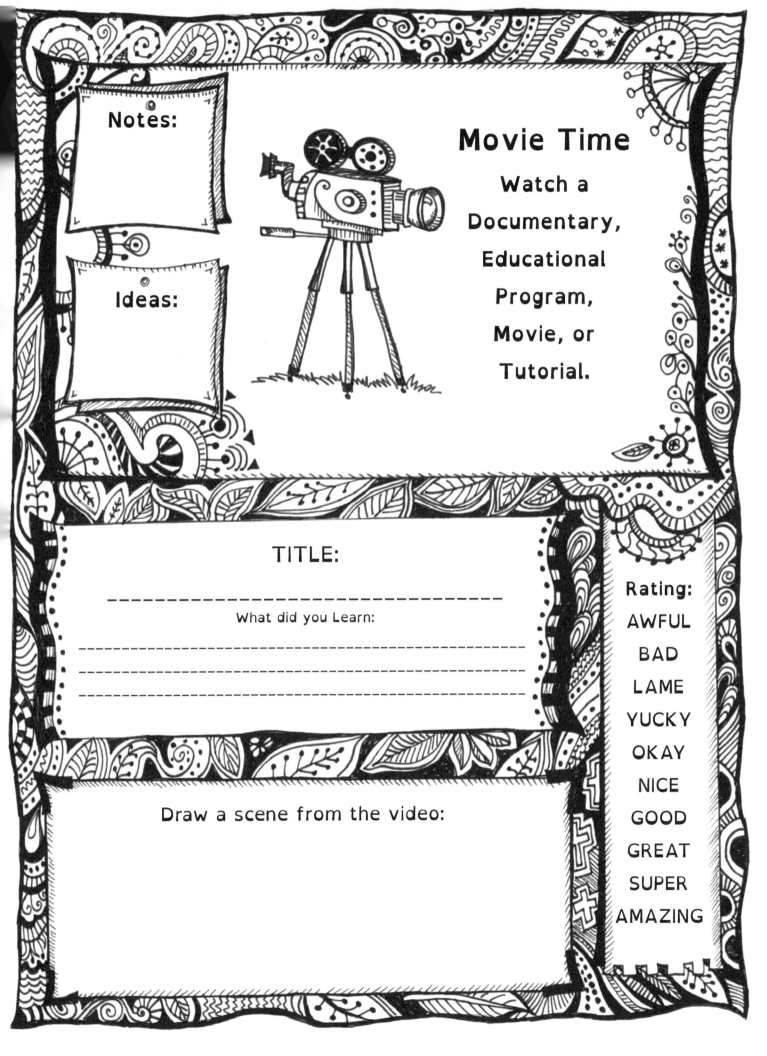

Notes:

Ideas:

Movie Time

Watch a Documentary, Educational Program, Movie, or Tutorial.

TITLE:

_____

What did you Learn:

_____
_____
_____

Draw a scene from the video:

Rating:

AWFUL

BAD

LAME

YUCKY

OKAY

NICE

GOOD

GREAT

SUPER

AMAZING

CIRCLE TODAY'S DATE

January
February
March
April
May
June
July
August
September
October
November
December

1 2 3 4 5 6
7 8 9 10 11
12 13 14 15
16 17 18 19
20 21 22 23
24 25 26 27
28 29 30 31

MONDAY
TUESDAY
WEDNESDAY
THURSDAY
FRIDAY
SATURDAY
SUNDAY

2018
2019
2020
2021
2022
2023
2024
2025
2026
2027
2028
2029
2030
2031

Write Today's Date: _ _ _ _ _ _ _ _ _ _ _ _ _ _ _ _

FEELINGS, PLANS & THOUGHTS

Copy a Quote or Verse:

_____

_____

_____

_____

_____

_____

Draw a picture about your feelings:

To-Do List

_____

_____

_____

_____

_____

MATH & CREATIVITY

Use this page for math problems
or design something like a house, farm or stable!

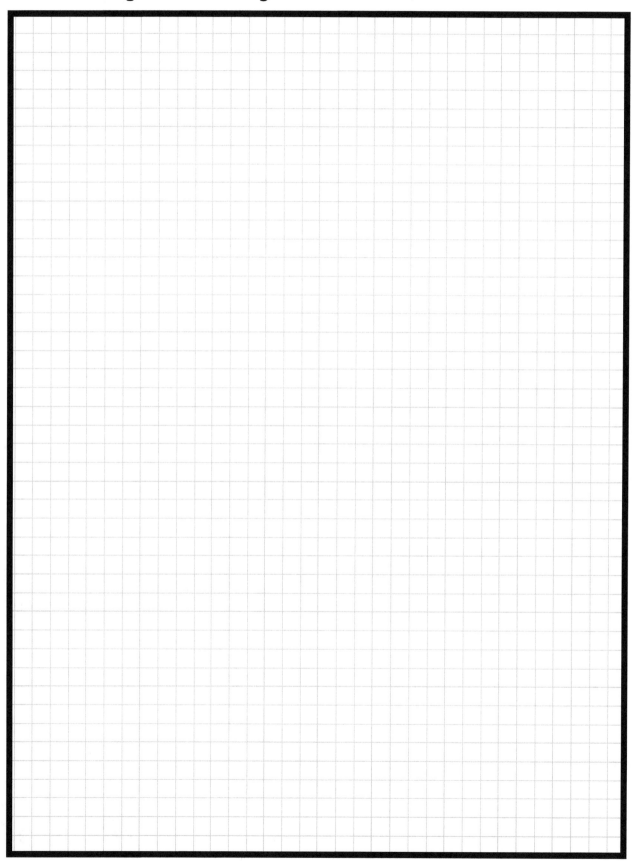

Listening Time

Listen to an audio book or classical music or ask someone to read a story to you while you color and draw on the next page.

What are you listening to?

_____

Create a Comic Strip!

CIRCLE TODAY'S DATE

January
February
March
April
May
June
July
August
September
October
November
December

1 2 3 4 5 6
7 8 9 10 11
12 13 14 15
16 17 18 19
20 21 22 23
24 25 26 27
28 29 30 31

MONDAY
TUESDAY
WEDNESDAY
THURSDAY
FRIDAY
SATURDAY
SUNDAY

2018
2019
2020
2021
2022
2023
2024
2025
2026
2027
2028
2029
2030
2031

Write Today's Date:_ _ _ _ _ _ _ _ _ _ _ _ _

FEELINGS, PLANS & THOUGHTS

Copy a Quote or Verse:

_____

_____

_____

_____

_____

_____

Draw a picture
about your feelings:

To-Do List

_____

_____

_____

_____

_____

_____

NATURE STUDY

Go outside and make a realistic drawing
of something you find in nature.

Reading Time - 1 Hour (Set a Timer)

Choose Four Books - Read from each book for 15 minutes.

Copy important words and pictures from your books:

Spelling Time

Find 20 Words with 7 letters each.
Look in your books for words.
Write the words here:

Notes:

Ideas:

Movie Time

Watch a Documentary, Educational Program, Movie, or Tutorial.

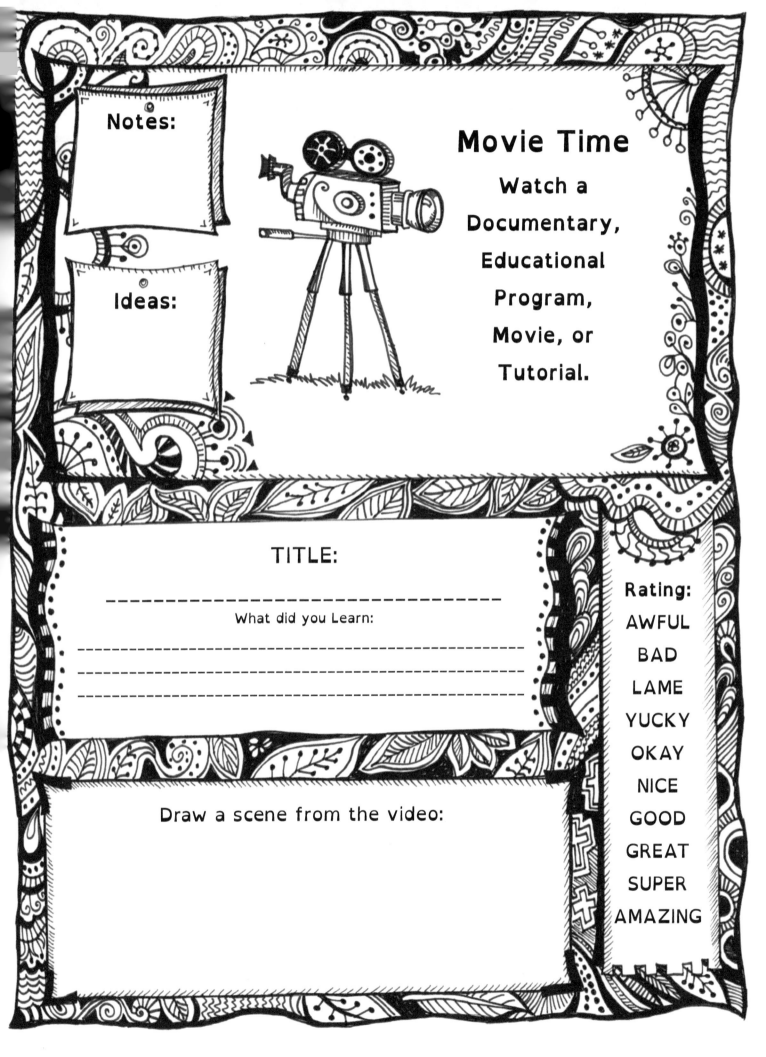

TITLE:

_____

What did you Learn:

_____
_____
_____

Draw a scene from the video:

Rating:
AWFUL
BAD
LAME
YUCKY
OKAY
NICE
GOOD
GREAT
SUPER
AMAZING

MATH & CREATIVITY

Use this page for math problems
or design something like a house, farm or stable!

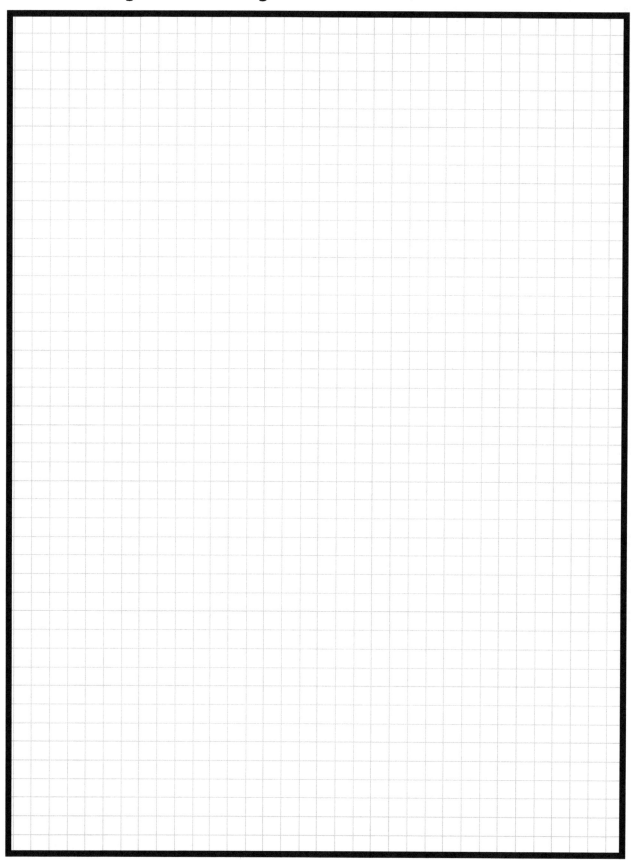

Fun Writing Practice:

ABCDEFGHIJKLMNOPQURSTUVWXYZ

abcdefghijklmnopqrstuvwxyz

ABCDEFGHIJKLMNOPQURSTUVWXYZ

ABCDEFGHIJKLMNOPQURSTUVWXYZ

abcdefghijklmnopqrstuvwxyz

ALL ABOUT HORSES:

Choose a Horse Breed to Research:

_____

List Four Facts about this Breed:

1._____
_____
2._____
_____
3._____
_____
4._____
_____

DRAW THIS TYPE OF HORSE OR TAPE A PICTURE HERE:

Create a Comic Strip!

CIRCLE TODAY'S DATE

January
February
March
April
May
June
July
August
September
October
November
December

1 2 3 4 5 6
7 8 9 10 11
12 13 14 15
16 17 18 19
20 21 22 23
24 25 26 27
28 29 30 31

MONDAY
TUESDAY
WEDNESDAY
THURSDAY
FRIDAY
SATURDAY
SUNDAY

2018
2019
2020
2021
2022
2023
2024
2025
2026
2027
2028
2029
2030
2031

Write Today's Date: _ _ _ _ _ _ _ _ _ _ _ _ _ _ _

FEELINGS, PLANS & THOUGHTS

Copy a Quote or Verse:

_____

_____

_____

_____

_____

_____

Draw a picture about your feelings:

To-Do List

_____

_____

_____

_____

_____

_____

NATURE STUDY

Go outside and make a realistic drawing
of something you find in nature.

Reading Time - 1 Hour (Set a Timer)

Choose Four Books - Read from each book for 15 minutes.

Copy important words and pictures from your books:

Spelling Time

Find 20 Words with **8** letters each.

Look in your books for words.

Write the words here:

_____   _____

_____   _____

_____   _____

_____   _____

_____   _____

_____   _____

_____   _____

_____   _____

_____   _____

Notes:

Ideas:

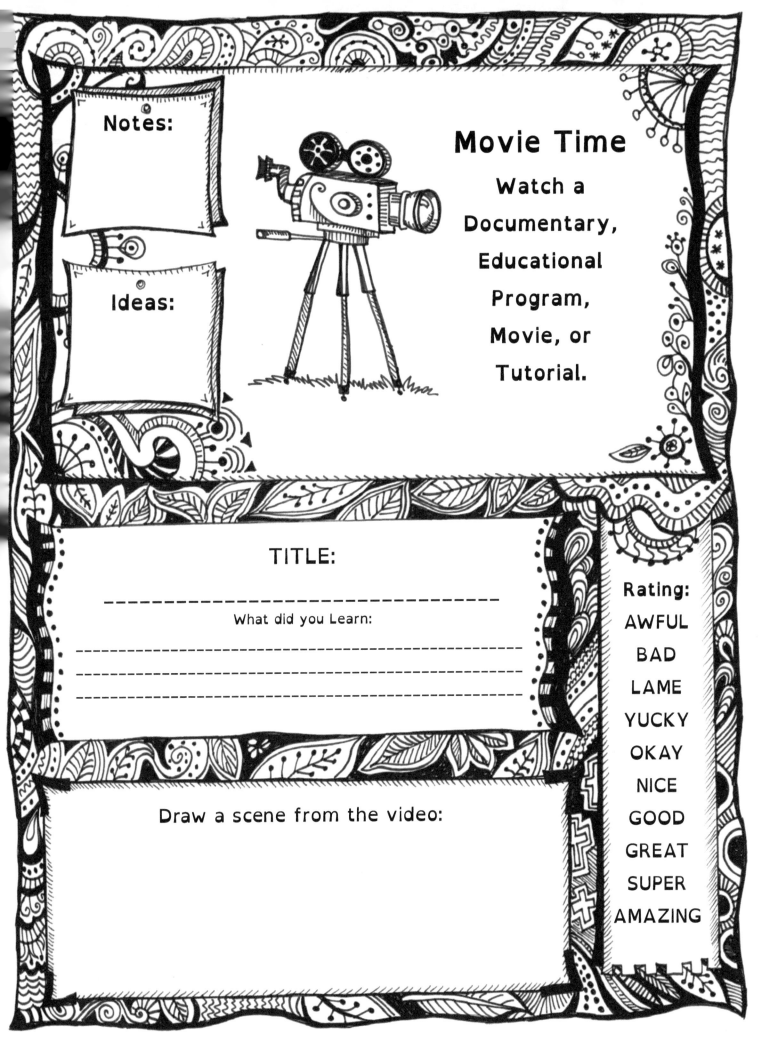

Movie Time

Watch a Documentary, Educational Program, Movie, or Tutorial.

TITLE:

_____

What did you Learn:

_____
_____
_____

Draw a scene from the video:

Rating:
AWFUL
BAD
LAME
YUCKY
OKAY
NICE
GOOD
GREAT
SUPER
AMAZING

MATH & CREATIVITY

Use this page for math problems
or design something like a house, farm or stable!

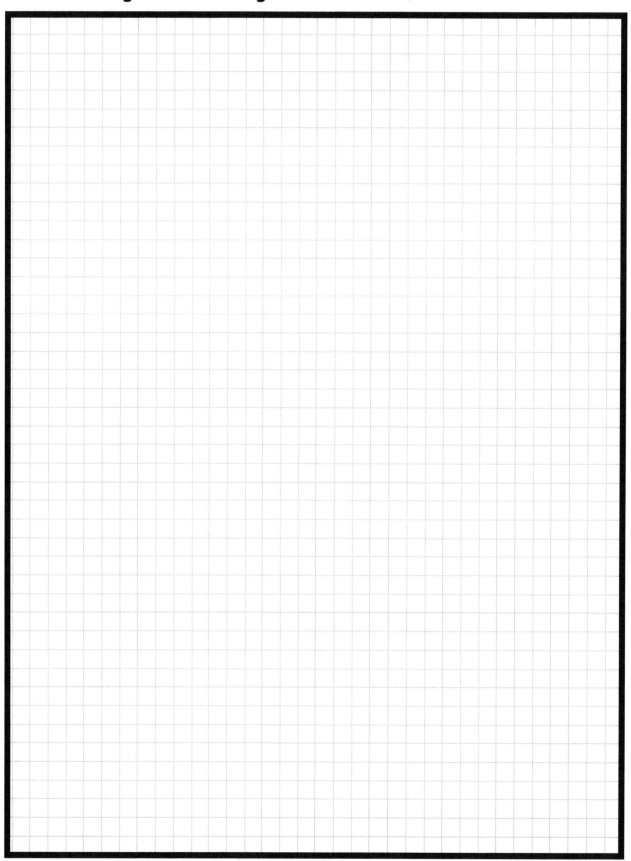

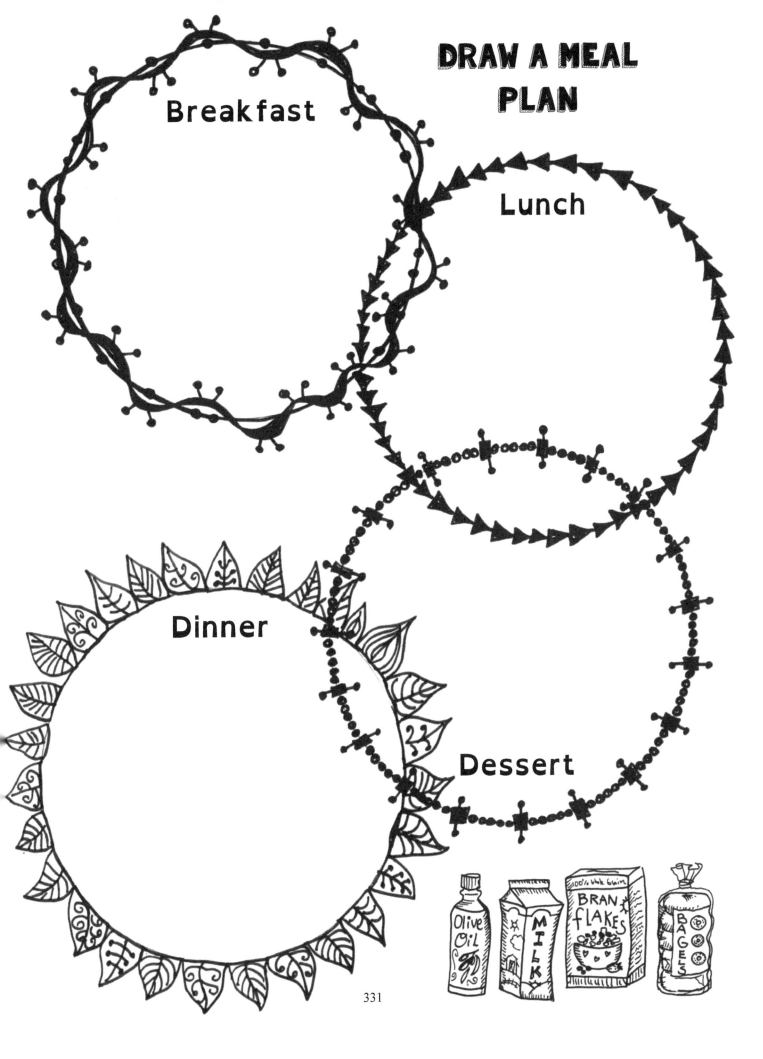

Breakfast

DRAW A MEAL PLAN

Lunch

Dinner

Dessert

331

ALL ABOUT HORSES:

Choose a Horse Breed to Research:

_____

List Four Facts about this Breed:

1. _____
_____
2. _____
_____
3. _____
_____
4. _____
_____

DRAW THIS TYPE OF HORSE OR TAPE A PICTURE HERE:

My FUN Page

CIRCLE TODAY'S DATE

January
February
March
April
May
June
July
August
September
October
November
December

1 2 3 4 5 6
7 8 9 10 11
12 13 14 15
16 17 18 19
20 21 22 23
24 25 26 27
28 29 30 31

MONDAY
TUESDAY
WEDNESDAY
THURSDAY
FRIDAY
SATURDAY
SUNDAY

2018
2019
2020
2021
2022
2023
2024
2025
2026
2027
2028
2029
2030
2031

Write Today's Date: _ _ _ _ _ _ _ _ _ _ _ _ _

FEELINGS, PLANS & THOUGHTS

Copy a Quote or Verse:

_____

_____

_____

_____

_____

_____

Draw a picture
about your feelings:

To-Do List

_____

_____

_____

_____

_____

_____

Picture Study

Look closely at this picture.

Think about the lines and shadows.

Practice working with your colored pencils.

Draw the Missing Spot

Use a variety of smooth black drawing pens,
with fine points, to complete the picture.

NATURE STUDY

Go outside and make a realistic drawing
of something you find in nature.

Reading Time - 1 Hour (Set a Timer)

Choose Four Books - Read from each book for 15 minutes.

Copy important words and pictures from your books:

Spelling Time

Find 20 Words with 7 letters each.
Look in your books for words.
Write the words here:

_____   _____

_____   _____

_____   _____

_____   _____

_____   _____

_____   _____

_____   _____

_____   _____

_____   _____

_____   _____

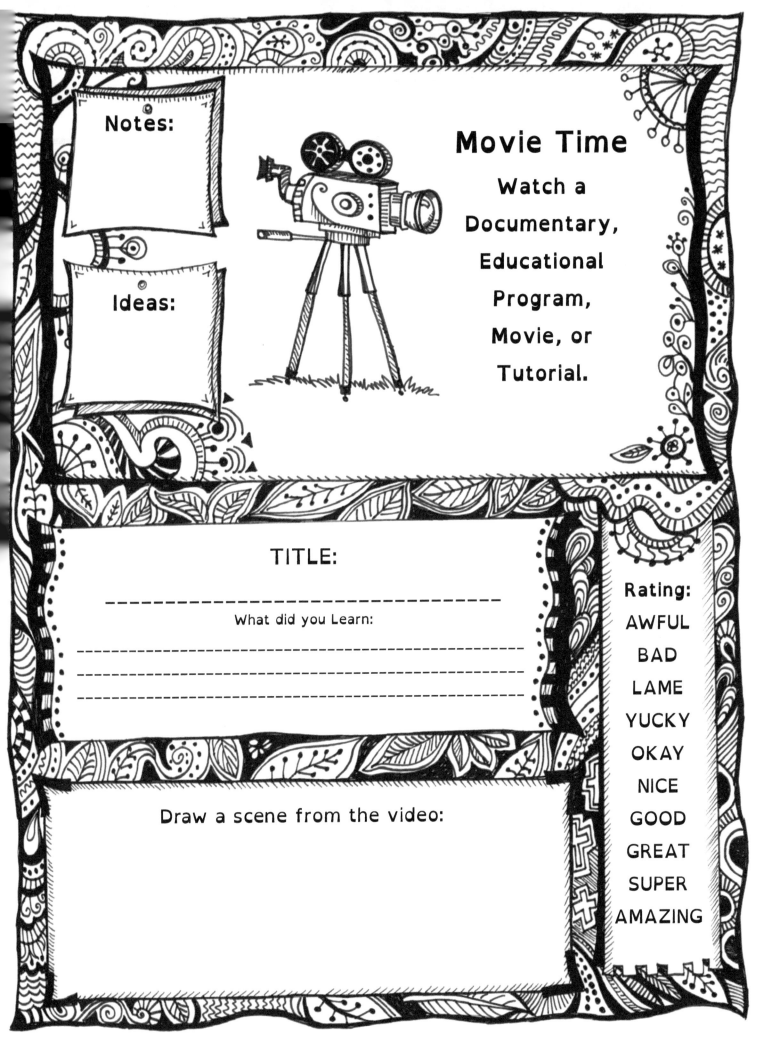

Notes:

Ideas:

Movie Time

Watch a Documentary, Educational Program, Movie, or Tutorial.

TITLE:

What did you Learn:

Draw a scene from the video:

Rating:
AWFUL
BAD
LAME
YUCKY
OKAY
NICE
GOOD
GREAT
SUPER
AMAZING

MATH & CREATIVITY

Use this page for math problems
or design something like a house, farm or stable!

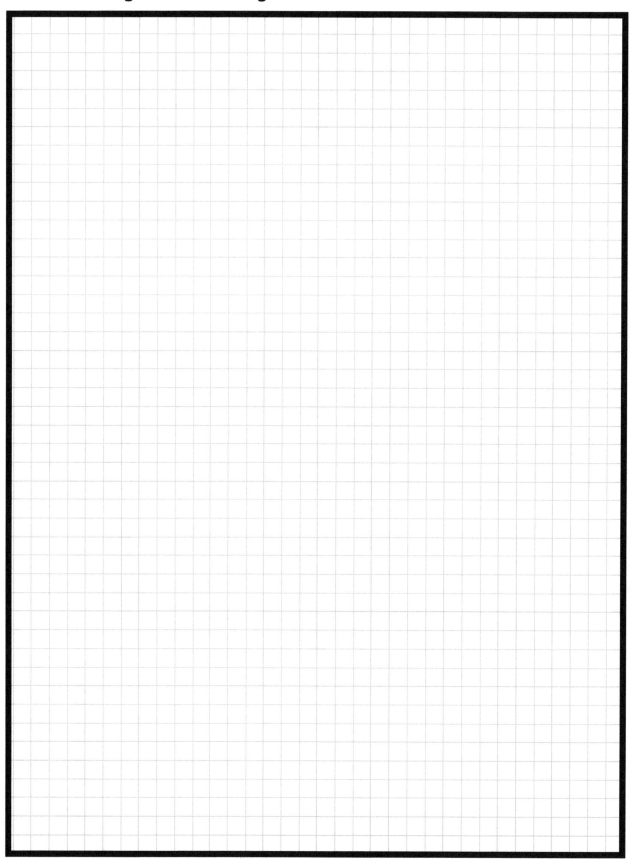

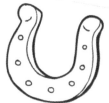

ALL ABOUT HORSES:

Choose a Horse Breed to Research:

_____

List Four Facts about this Breed:

1. _____
_____
2. _____
_____
3. _____
_____
4. _____
_____

DRAW THIS TYPE OF HORSE OR TAPE A PICTURE HERE:

CIRCLE TODAY'S DATE

January
February
March
April
May
June
July
August
September
October
November
December

1 2 3 4 5 6
7 8 9 10 11
12 13 14 15
16 17 18 19
20 21 22 23
24 25 26 27
28 29 30 31

MONDAY
TUESDAY
WEDNESDAY
THURSDAY
FRIDAY
SATURDAY
SUNDAY

2018
2019
2020
2021
2022
2023
2024
2025
2026
2027
2028
2029
2030
2031

Write Today's Date: _ _ _ _ _ _ _ _ _ _ _ _ _ _

FEELINGS, PLANS & THOUGHTS

Copy a Quote or Verse:

_____

_____

_____

_____

_____

_____

Draw a picture about your feelings:

To-Do List

_____

_____

_____

_____

_____

_____

NATURE STUDY

Go outside and make a realistic drawing
of something you find in nature.

Reading Time - 1 Hour (Set a Timer)

Choose Four Books - Read from each book for 15 minutes.

Copy important words and pictures from your books:

Spelling Time

Find 20 Words with 7 letters each.

Look in your books for words.

Write the words here:

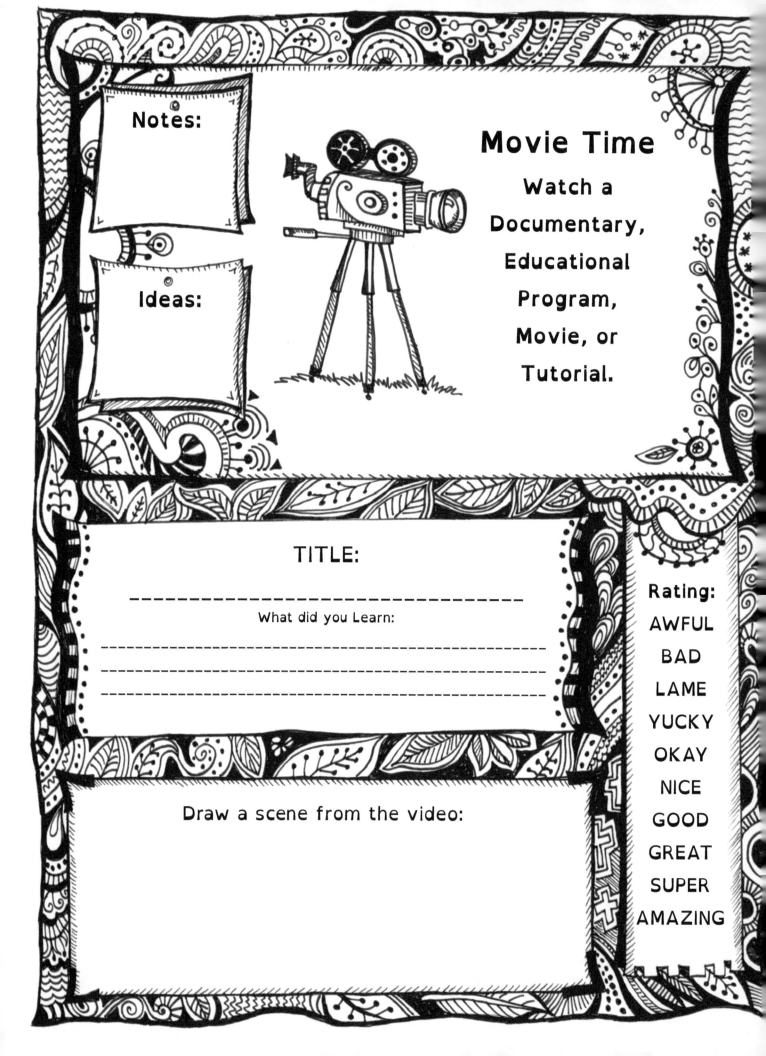

Notes:

Ideas:

Movie Time
Watch a Documentary, Educational Program, Movie, or Tutorial.

TITLE:

_____

What did you Learn:

_____
_____
_____

Rating:

AWFUL

BAD

LAME

YUCKY

OKAY

NICE

GOOD

GREAT

SUPER

AMAZING

Draw a scene from the video:

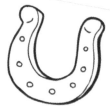

ALL ABOUT HORSES:

Choose a Horse Breed to Research:

_____

List Four Facts about this Breed:

1._____
_____

2._____
_____

3._____
_____

4._____
_____

DRAW THIS TYPE OF HORSE OR TAPE A PICTURE HERE:

Create a Comic Strip!

CIRCLE TODAY'S DATE

January
February
March
April
May
June
July
August
September
October
November
December

1 2 3 4 5 6
7 8 9 10 11
12 13 14 15
16 17 18 19
20 21 22 23
24 25 26 27
28 29 30 31

MONDAY
TUESDAY
WEDNESDAY
THURSDAY
FRIDAY
SATURDAY
SUNDAY

2018
2019
2020
2021
2022
2023
2024
2025
2026
2027
2028
2029
2030
2031

Write Today's Date:_ _ _ _ _ _ _ _ _ _ _ _ _ _

FEELINGS, PLANS & THOUGHTS

Copy a Quote or Verse:

_____

_____

_____

_____

_____

_____

Draw a picture
about your feelings:

To-Do List

_____

_____

_____

_____

_____

Picture Study

Look closely at this picture.

Think about the lines and shadows.

Practice working with your colored pencils.

Draw the Missing Spot

Use a variety of smooth black drawing pens,
with fine points, to complete the picture.

NATURE STUDY

Go outside and make a realistic drawing
of something you find in nature.

Reading Time - 1 Hour (Set a Timer)

Choose Four Books - Read from each book for 15 minutes.

Copy important words and pictures from your books:

Spelling Time

Find 20 Words with 10 letters each.
Look in your books for words.
Write the words here:

Notes:

Ideas:

Movie Time

Watch a Documentary, Educational Program, Movie, or Tutorial.

TITLE:

_____

What did you Learn:

_____
_____
_____

Draw a scene from the video:

Rating:

AWFUL

BAD

LAME

YUCKY

OKAY

NICE

GOOD

GREAT

SUPER

AMAZING

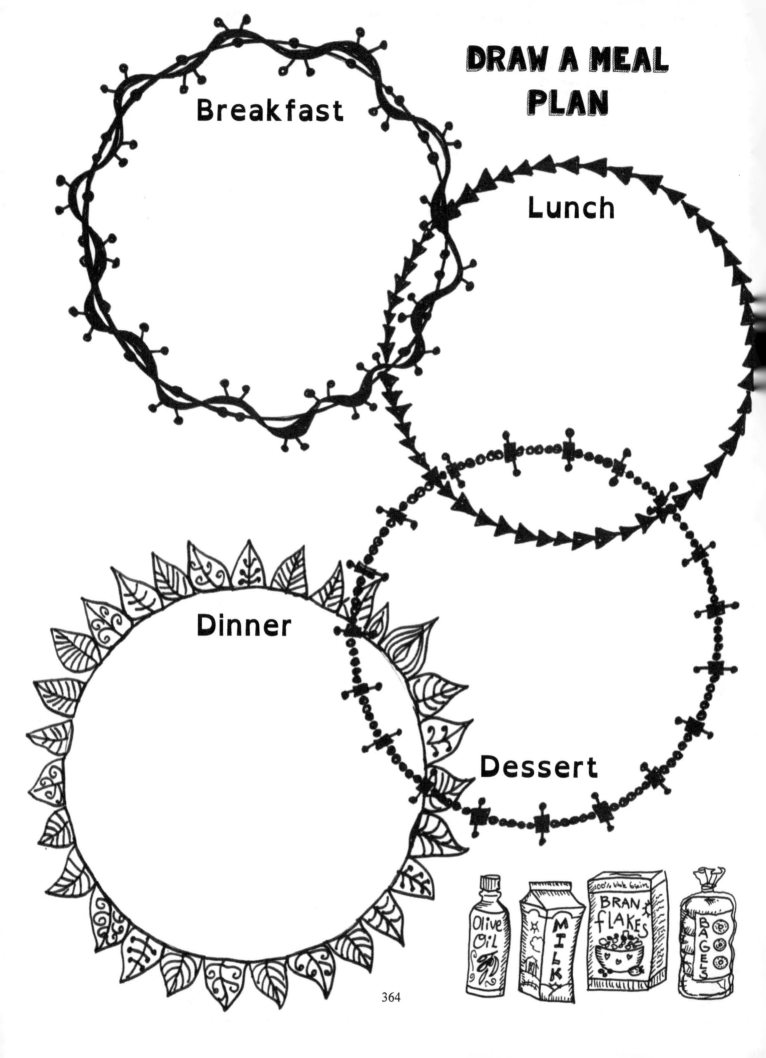

Breakfast

Lunch

Dinner

Dessert

DRAW A MEAL PLAN

364

ALL ABOUT HORSES:

Choose a Horse Breed to Research:

_____

List Four Facts about this Breed:

1._____
_____
2._____
_____
3._____
_____
4._____
_____

DRAW THIS TYPE OF HORSE OR TAPE A PICTURE HERE:

My FUN Page

MATH & CREATIVITY

Use this page for math problems
or design something like a house, farm or stable!

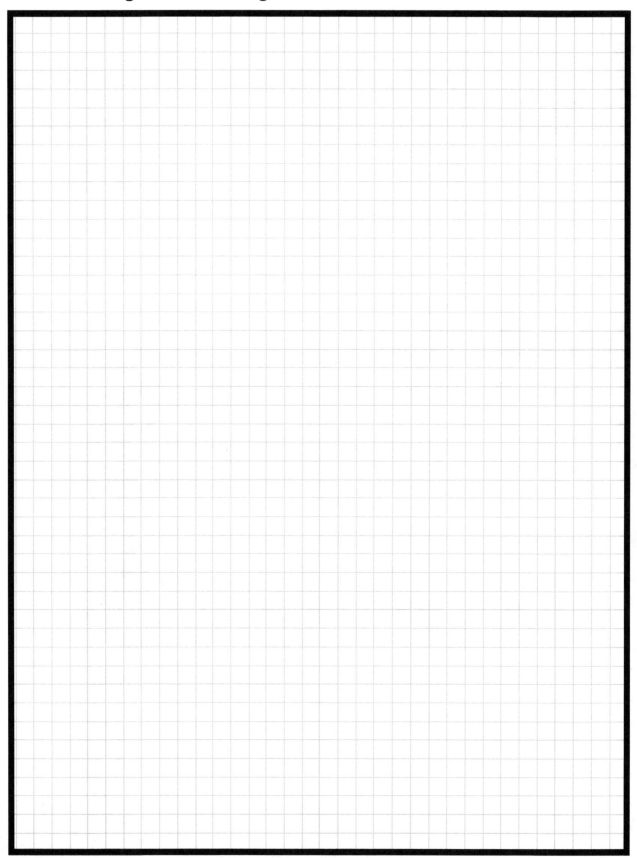

Picture Study

Look closely at this picture.

Think about the lines and shadows.

Practice working with your colored pencils.

Create a Comic Strip!

Do It Yourself
HOMESCHOOL
JOURNALS

Made in United States
Troutdale, OR
07/24/2023

11517763R00206